Notes from a Postman

A Collection of Poems, Thoughts, and Prayers

Robert,
   God be with you my friend.
      Jonathan C. Hyatt
         Zeph. 3:17

Written by

Jonathan C. Hyatt

Edited by Rosanna Neynaber

The content and views expressed in this book are those of the author and do not necessarily represent those of the United States Postal Service.

Dedication

For my Lord and Savior, Jesus Christ,

To my dear wife, Camille, and for all my family,

To my church family and friends,

And to all my postal customers

DESCRIPTION OF BOOK

Notes from a Postman - A Collection of Poems, Thoughts, and Prayers is an inspirational book based upon the spiritual journey of the author, Jonathan C. Hyatt, as a Christian youth and throughout his adulthood. As a youth, Jonathan learns to unlock his heart by writing his thoughts and prayers in his letters to God. However, as a young man, life soon gets busy for Hyatt and he rarely finds the inspiration to write. His letters remain saved, tucked away, in a cedar chest, almost forgotten. Several years pass, and his pen remains silent. At long last, through the spontaneous kindness of a young boy named Abel, Hyatt receives his inspiration to write once again. Suddenly, he begins to write his thoughts, reflections and prayers intertwined with passages from the Bible which speak to his heart. Throughout his own personal struggles, and his wife Camille's battle with cancer, Jonathan learns that God is very near to the humble and broken hearted. Encouraged by his family and friends, Hyatt's writing collection becomes a book, which he hopes will inspire many people.

Contents

About the Author

Written by his mother, Charlene Hyatt
Given to Jon on his 50th birthday on 11/27/19

In 1969, on a Thanksgiving morn,
Our son, Jonathan Carl Hyatt, was born.
He wasn't a turkey right from the start
And found his way quickly into our hearts.
With big blue eyes and soft blond hair,
He rather seemed to not have a single care.
Mom's buddy when the rest were away,
He was her "little lover boy," she'd say.
Being outside was where he liked to be,
Riding a bike, hiking, or climbing a tree.
He loved our dog Shandon very much
And used her for a comfy pillow and such.
He did lots of yard work to earn some bucks
And saved enough money to buy his first truck.
He made a few trips to the ER, and there soon
Told his worried mom to go out of the room.
He loved to dress up and spend time on his hair.
This pleased the church ladies when he was there.
He liked to sing, memorize verses, and be in plays.
He sang in school choir and in church gave praise.
In high school choir, he met Camille, his future wife.
Later, two sons, Brandon and Nicholas, filled their life.
Jon delivers mail for the USPS and does great there,
And customers think highly of him 'cause he shows he cares.
At Christmas, he receives lots of money, gifts and cards.
When he's off and is back, they're happy to see him in their yards.
Jon's favorite place to shop is Costco, taking samples along the way.
He wanted to have his 50th birthday there but will wait for another day.
These past 50 years with our son Jon have blessed our hearts.
We pray for many more years and blessings as this day we mark.

Love, Mom and Dad

The Mailman's Prayer

I got a letter from you, Lord; come and guide me today.
Send me a message from heaven; come and show me the way.
People all around me are dying, rejecting you day by day.
Give me your stories to tell them; help me to point to your way.
I got a letter from heaven; I know you more, and I know now what to say.
Lord, I don't want to scare them; come speak your words into my heart today,
Each word coming down from Jesus; open up my mouth Lord, open it today.
I got a letter from heaven; come wash my feet with it today.
Wash all of me, Lord, I want to say.
Your stories flood my heart; I want to tell them the way.
I need my brothers and sisters to pray, to come before your throne room and say,
To be your hands and be your feet, to walk with you, Lord, walking day by day.
Tell them all about your story, giving them something you say.
You are my Mailman, Jesus; only you call me a son by my name.
Help us deliver your message and not seek after worldly fame.
I want to put my hand into your side, to see your nail prints today.
I want my eyes to be like your eyes, because I'm going to see you someday.
Help me, Lord, to walk like Enoch did, to go an extra mile for you today;
He's falling down, before the Throne of God, casting his crown to you, each day.
I say this prayer on bended knee, Lord. Please clean up my heart today.
Make it pure and holy. Make it like yours, I pray.
You're going to send us revival! You're coming back to our town one day.
Jesus, finish your story, "To God Be the Glory," I pray.
Make us into mailmen like you, Jesus, with a small letter "m."
When they say "yes" to your calling, angels will be saying "A-men!"

1
The Early Years

Seven Letters to God

When I was a young teenager, I began to write some letters to God. These letters helped me to express my feelings to the Lord. I learned that I could tell God anything going on in my life and that he would listen to me. My relationship with the Lord began to grow stronger. Like the Psalmist David, I learned how to cry out to the Lord.

1. Dear God,
    I want you to know that I love you! Thanks for everything. Please help everything to work out cool. You know what I mean. I love you, Jesus! I pray that the lesson me and Greg present will influence everyone and be a great lesson. You're the Greatest God. Fill me with your Spirit every day and wash me in your blood. I look forward to seeing you, Dad and Buddy!!
    Later,
    Amen
    Love,
    Jonathan Hyatt

2. Jesus, you are worthy to be praised. You make the difference in my life. I love you, guy. You're a true friend. Many times I'm lost, and I don't know where to turn. It's nice to turn to you. You always rescue me. I want to serve you, Friend. Send me where you want me to go. I'm in your hands. I trust in you alone, my God! How can I ever repay you? Lead me, Lord, show me the way. I believe in you!! I love you, Buddy! Take it easy up there. Say hello to Gramps for me. Tell him it won't be too much longer and we'll be joining him. Later, Dudes.
    Love,
    Jonathan
    P.S. Help me to live up to my name, and always be a friend to anyone who needs me. You were to me. Luv Ya!

3. Lord,
    If I could ask one thing from you, and you would give that wish to me, no matter what it is, I would ask for wisdom. I believe this gift would be far better than anything else. In so many ways, I see myself as Solomon. I am a leader, and I have a great love for women just like him, but I also want to serve you. With this wisdom, I could be the right kind of leader and make the right decisions. I can't rely on my own knowledge, God. I need you. We talked about wisdom last night, at our youth meeting. I learned that we are like fools in our own knowledge compared to you. All of the good talents in my life aren't because of me, they are from you. God, I don't care about being great, and you know what my goals are.

I feel that if I had just a speck of your wisdom, I could make the right decisions, and help others too. I want to serve you...

God, I love you! I look forward to walking and talking with you. I'll be free...please help this change to start in my heart. God, I believe in you and trust in you. Draw me closer and closer to you until we see each other, face to face; then we shall never die. Nothing can stop us.

Later, Bud,

Jonathan

P.S. A-men

4. Jon Hyatt's Psalm to God

   I once was lost, and a slave to sin, but your power set me free, within. Oh lord, my God, you are my Refuge and Strength. You set me free and unlocked the doors. You said you would never leave me nor forsake me, Lord. Help me, to never leave you. In times of trouble, I will call on your name for help, because I know you will always listen and deliver me. You are my God, oh Lord, and I am your servant. Fill me with your Spirit each day and give me wisdom. Help me to draw closer to you, and never surrender. Help me to use my gifts to the fullest, oh Lord, and always call upon your name. I will give you thanks, praise, and adoration, oh Lord, because I once was lost, and a slave to sin, BUT YOU FOUND ME and set me free from within.

   A-men

5. Jesus,

   When the nights are so long, and I can't seem to sleep, I remember you and what you have given me. You have given me love and trust I can keep. Without you, I would be lost, like a stone in the sea. You are my Friend, and I know you care. You always listen, and you're always there. You're ready to teach me and show me the way. To keep me from danger, in your arms I'll stay. Yes, you are my Friend...you are a Brother, and your love will never end. You're my Father. You're everything I will always need. Jesus, you mean everything to me!

   Jonathan

6. Dear God,

   "Father, forgive them; for they know not what they're doing." "Father, into Thy hands I commit my Spirit."

   It is finished. It is done, the work of God's only Son. The war has been won! You are a witness of these things. Go and proclaim his name. This world will never be the same, because I've taken the blame.

   Dare to be different, dare to take a stand. It's either hot or cold, and this kind of love can't be sold.

   It is finished. It is done, the work of God's only son. The war has been won! The war has been won!! The war has been won!!! Been Won!!!!!! Jonathan

   Luke 23:34&46, Matthew 28:18-20, 1 Corinthians 15:3-4, Revelation 3:15

7. Dear Lord, July 22, '87,
   11:23 P.M.

I feel an emptiness inside. I feel all alone. I can't help but feel this way. I feel like all my "friends" have deserted me. But God, I know you are here. You will never leave me. Many times, like now, I am confused and I don't know what to believe. This is the time I cast all worries and doubts away, and I place my faith in you, my Heavenly Father. Only you know what is best, because your will is best. God, I pray that your will would be done in my life. God, I can feel that it is your will for me to go to camp. I need that time away to concentrate on you. Last year, camp was tough, but I grew closer to you and gained trust in you. I believe in you, God, and I trust in you, and I will try not to worry about things that bother me. I place my trust in you. You see, I need you, Jesus, and I wouldn't make it if you weren't by my side. I want to serve you and obey you. Help me to always be strong and not to give in to temptations. Again, if I could just ask one thing of you, and leave you at that, I ask for your Holy Spirit's wisdom to overflow in my life, and make me like you.

FAITH "Lord, make me like you, Lord, please make me like you.

You are a servant, make me one too. Oh Lord, I am willing, do what you must do.

To make me like you, Lord, just make me like you."

(Worship song: "Lord, Make Me Like You")

I love you Jesus! Love, Jonathan C. Hyatt. A True Believer!!!

Early Songs

JESUS, I Just...
4/13/90

Vs1:   There's a man that I know, and he'll never let you down.

         He's the only True Friend that I have ever found.

Vs2:   He was nailed to a cross, where He died for you and me.

         He said, "Father, forgive them," as he hung upon the tree.

Chorus: Jesus, I just want to thank you, for dying at Calvary.

             Jesus, I just want to praise you; I'm gonna sing for eternity.

Vs3:   They laid Him in a tomb, but He rose on the third day.

         This world won't be the same, 'cause the stone was rolled away.

Chorus: Jesus, I just want to thank you, for dying at Calvary.

             Jesus, I just want to praise you; I'm gonna sing for eternity.

Repeat: I thank you, Lord, yes, I praise you, but I still love you even more.

             So Jesus, I'm just gonna serve you, gonna serve you forevermore.

Would You Let Me Know

3/25/89

Vs1:   If I could write a song for you, I'd sing it till I die, I'd sing it till I die.
        If I could explain the way I feel, it wouldn't be a lie...

Vs2:   If I could be your friend, I'd never let you down, I'd never let you down.
        If I could say a prayer for you, I'd pray it every day...

Chorus: Because when I look into your eyes, my heart cannot let go;
               My heart just can't let go.
               And when I think about you, Girl, a smile comes on my face...

Vs3:   If I could give you anything, it wouldn't be enough, it wouldn't be enough.
        If I could ask you how you feel, would you let me know?

Chorus: Because when I look into your eyes, my heart just can't let go;
               My heart just can't let go.
               And when I think about you, Girl, a smile comes on my face.
               And all my fears in this world suddenly vanish without a trace...

        Would you let me know?

"Daniel" was written on 11/02/90 in memory of my dear friend. Daniel and his brother, Aaron, loved to play in the back of my Ford pickup truck, at church. I always enjoyed wrestling with them and horsing around. Daniel was around six years old when he passed away in a car accident. This song was recorded and played at his service. My friend, Keith, helped me put it to music. During the recording, Keith played the guitar and I did the vocals. Camille, my girlfriend, and future wife, attended the service with me.

DANIEL

V1:   Daniel's in the sky, 'cause Jesus took him home.
        He was a friend of mine, but I know he's not alone.

Chorus: He's singing songs to Jesus and walking streets of gold.
               There's not a tear in his eye, 'cause Daniel's in the sky.

Vs2:   I often wonder why a little child goes?
        But in this heart of mine, I know he's doing fine.

Chorus: He's singing songs to Jesus and walking streets of gold.
               There's not a tear in his eye, 'cause Daniel's in the sky.

VISIONS
11/22/86

Vs1: Visions of endless love lie captured in my mind.
Pictures of painted dreams, lost in time.
Sometimes love can hurt, sometimes love prevails.
But His love always heals.

Vs2: You are my destiny, you are my prize…
A long-awaited fantasy, found through time.
Tonight I live my dream; tonight I sing my song.
Tonight I love you; tomorrow could be gone…

Chorus: You are the one I've waited for, for so long…
I surrender my love to you.
Forever, always forever, you'll be…my never-ending song.

Vs3: What will our future bring? What will the next line be?
One promise I give to you, only time will see.

EASTER SONG
Matthew 23-24 & Luke 24:50-51
3/26/89

Vs1: They nailed him to a cross, where he died for you and me.
He said, "Father, forgive them," as he hung upon the tree.
They laid him in a tomb, but He rose on the third day.
Two women looked for him, but the stone was rolled away.

Chorus: He picks me up when I fall, and he carries me through it all.
He listens to me when I call. My Father's watching over me.
He listens to me when I call. My Father's watching over me.

Vs2: He said, "Do not be afraid, go and take word
To my friends in Galilee, 'cause that's where they'll see Me."
He lifted up his hands, and he blessed all of them.
The disciples looked up at him, as he rose to heaven.

Chorus

Bridge: Would you accept my Lord? He really loves you so.
I'd like to pray with you, so you can let him know.

Chorus

13

7 NUMBERS
Dedicated to "Stan the Man"
9/8/89

Vs1:   If you need someone to hold your hand
If you need someone who understands
Someone to lean on the times you almost fall
Someone who listens each moment you call

Chorus: Just dial seven numbers and ask for the Lord
He'll take any numbers, just ask for the Lord

Vs2:   There's a deadline you have to meet
You're running out of time, you're at the boss' feet
You've tried everything and there's no way out
But there's someone who you haven't thought about

Chorus: Just dial seven numbers and ask for the Lord
He'll take any numbers, just ask for the Lord

Vs3:   You're going crazy, looking for a date
Asking every boy or girl, no time to wait
Take it slow, and give it some time
Pick up the phone, get the Lord on the line

Chorus: Just dial seven numbers and ask for the Lord
He'll take any numbers, just ask for the Lord.

Vs4:   Life is too short to worry about the day
Always remember, DON'T FORGET TO PRAY!
He's never too busy, and He wants to talk to you
He's never too busy; He'll show you what to do

LOVE SONG

Vs1:   Sometimes I think of her and realize: Tonight is the night we must say goodbye.
          Will I ever see her, or will our love just die? What will happen? I lay and cry.

Chorus: She will always be in my thoughts forever,
          And maybe someday we shall be together.
          Whispering the words, I love you.
          Tonight is the night we will remember.
          Tonight is the night we begin forever.

Vs2:   But as I lay here, I realize this is all a dream.
          Why must I awake, I cry? Now I really want to die.

Vs3:   But as I look outside, I see that star,
          Still shining and twinkling from afar.
          Our love will always shine forever,
          And someday I will find that star.

Chorus: She will always be in my thoughts forever,
          And maybe someday we shall be together.
          Whispering the words, I love you.
          Tonight is the night we will remember.
          Tonight is the night we begin forever.

Bridge: As I look, I don't believe my eyes! That star is shining in my room.
          And suddenly, I realize that star is you!!!

Chorus: She will always be in my thoughts forever,
          And maybe someday we shall be together.
          Whispering the words, I love you.
          Tonight is the night we will remember.
          Tonight is the night we begin forever.

          Tonight is the night we will remember.
          Tonight is the night we begin forever.
          Whispering the words, I love you…

SOMEONE WHO CARES

Jon Hyatt (vocals) & Keith (vocals and guitar)

Vs1: On a cool, dark evening, as I was lying in my bed,
Memories of the past still captured in my head,
I was thinking about love, the good times that we had.
Will I ever see them again?

Vs2: People all around me, listening to the lies,
Not knowing where truth is, another baby dies.
Our world is so selfish; no one takes a stand.
Who will be the one to lend a hand?

Chorus 1: But I know someone who cares;
With His love He'll wipe away your tears.
He's the one that I call Jesus, He's the one for you.
He's the one that I call Jesus, He's the one for you.

Vs3: He loves you so much that He died for you.
What He did no other man can do.
Will you accept Him? Can you call Him Lord?
He is waiting for you. Will you open up the door?

Chorus 2: 'Cause I know someone who cares;
With His love He'll wipe away your tears.
He's the one that I call Jesus, He's the one for you.
He's the one that I call Jesus, He's the one for you.

Early Poems

Her beauty is very rare, and she knows how much I care,
Because my love for her will always be there.
And we'll live in communion as one,
And our love will keep shining like the sun.

THE MORNING BREEZE

Like the morning breeze and the sound of spring,
I think of her and the warmth of her voice.
For I know that someday she will bring all her love, and I will rejoice,
Because a love like that is hard to find,
And a love like that will fill my space inside.
How could I be so blind?
But I am still looking, and I will know when I see her face.

BEHIND EVERY STORM
3/21/91

There's a rainbow coloring the mountains.
A dark sky becomes blue, and the clouds disappear.
The sparrow sings her song, and the blades of grass stand tall.
God paints the picture, and His creation remembers the promise given to us all.

FRIENDS

There's one life to live, and one song to sing,
But there is nothing more special than the love God brings.
He sends us friends that care and share.
These friends help us with the problems we bear.
There is nothing more meaningful than a smile
And a friend that is always there.
For if we're alone, who is there to care?
But if you are alone, I will always be there.
If you are down, I'll be ready to care,
Because friends share this love and stick together.
And from this, they will always be friends, and live forever.

THE CRUSH
To Michele B. (1/14/88) and Adriana (2/27/89)
Praise God, they both rejected me!

One stormy night, as I lay in my bed
Sweet moments of yesterday, captured in my head
Visions of you and I, walking along the sand
Watching the sunset, hand in hand
Your long hair blowing through the wind
As the waves crash and the sun goes down
No other man could even comprehend a woman like you to be found

HEARTACHE

Many times, I remember this girl. I often dream of her by my side,
Her blond hair blowing in the breeze, her blue eyes reflecting the light,
Her soft skin carrying her smooth fragrance.
Sometimes I picture us as friends, sometimes as lovers, but can we be both?
I want her to know my feelings locked deep inside.
I want to show her just how much I care.
But now she is gone. I feel so lonely now, but I came too late.
I dream of how it could be, but I always wake up every day.
Days pass. How angry I am at him. How could he do this to her?
She returns heartbroken. All I can do is be there for her, to see her through the pain.
I am also happy, and somewhere inside, I still feel hope.
This time, I'll be ready, and this time I won't let her go.
 I'll show her how much I care.

To J.R. (2/9/88)

I met J.R. at camp. He played the piano, and we loved to hang out and sing together. One year, we had a talent show at my church, Windsor Hills. J.R. borrowed my black tux and I wore my white tux. We performed Michael W. Smith's song, "Friends are Friends Forever." J.R. played the piano, while we both sang and harmonized together.

You, you are my friend, the kind who gives me strength. You make me laugh and you make me cry. Our love will never die. 'Cause you pick me up when I fall, and you carry me in your arms and hold me tight. You, you are my friend, one I trust I can depend on. I think of you and I wonder why, some people don't even try. Give me your hand. Our love can take a stand. We are all his children; He will see us through, He will see us through, to the end. You, you are my friend. I wish I could be with you, but I know someday, our love will find a way, and we'll be together, it will be forever, in His arms. Give me your hand; our love must take a stand. We are all His children; He will see us through, He will see us through, He will see us through, to the end.

FREE
6/29/88

You want someone to trust, you need someone to care,
But please remember me, 'cause when you call I will be there,
To pick you up when you fall, to hold you like a doll,
'Cause you are my friend, and our love will never end.
You can trust in me, I will set you free,
'Cause you are my friend, and our love will never end.
You can trust in me, I will set you free.
As you start to dry your tears, you lose all of your fears,
And you turn your eyes to me, 'cause you know I will always be.
And that smile comes on your face, with that sparkle in your eyes.
No one could ever replace, we'll never have goodbyes.
'Cause you are my friend, and our love will never end.
You can trust in me, you can trust in me, 'cause I will set you free.
You want someone to trust, you need someone to care,
But please remember me; when you call, I will be there.

MOM

This poem is dedicated to my mother, Charlene. Her creative writing first inspired me to begin writing as a young man.

Many times I'm confused; I know not what to do.
These are the times I come to you.
You always know what's right, and the words to say.
You always seem to brighten my day.
Thanks for being there for me,
And thanks for that smile on your face,
A mother who will always be someone you can't replace.
In return, I shall give unto you simply what you have given me,
That love that shines through and through,
A love which will always be a lasting love forever.
Gee, Mom, ain't I clever? (Just kidding, Mom)

Early Story

PUT YOUR TRUST IN HIM

As I walked along the sand, I remembered a man. The man was sad and lonely, for he had lost someone whom he had deeply loved. The man had given everything he could to her, but then he lost her, and she didn't want to come home. For a long time he walked about, sad and lonely. He had forgotten Jesus, who had given His life for him. He had forgotten all the people that had walked out on Jesus and had even killed him. But as he walked along, he remembered God. He thought to himself, "I have left Jesus! No wonder I still hurt." That day he prayed, and the Lord heard his cry. Soon the pain was over. All he had to do was trust in God.

As he continued down the shores, he saw a young woman was crying. As she looked up, he remembered his pain. He told her about Jesus and what he had to go through. Soon her tears stopped, and she said, "I want to meet this Jesus." As they prayed, he realized this woman was the girl, the one he had lost. Then she said, "Daddy, I want to come home."

2

MY WIFE CAMILLE

MY FUTURE WIFE

As I sit back and think of the day, the memories of her come to my mind.
The beauty of her eyes seem to say: no other girl like her will I find.
Her heart is so happy, and it shows on her face.
She seems to always smile, no matter the place.
No person or thing could replace her, the girl I've waited for so long.
I know her not now, but when I see her she will say,
"I love you. I'll be with you all the way…"
Even when we die shall we be together, for our love is true; it shall last forever.
I shall always remember that girl, and someday she will come to me,
Making me the happiest man in the world!

CAMMIE (6/21/89)

I always thought I knew what love was, a strange feeling that no one understands.
There is something special that it does; I feel it when I touch your hands.
I always thought I could love somebody, a commitment that I would never break.
There is something meaningful it can be; it is a promise that you make.
I used to dream about the moment when I would never let you go.
I would tell you what love really meant, and I would always let you know.
I used to wonder about all of these things; what can love possibly do?
But I am certain of what it brings, and I feel it when I'm with you!

CAMMIE SAYS YES!

Vs1:   Wherever I go, whatever the place, I think about you, I see your face.
        I see your smile, I look in your eyes, they tell me secrets, and they never lie.

Vs2:   I see your lips, they whisper to me, I hear your voice, it never leaves me.
        I feel your kiss, a gentle caress, your arms around me, my heart tells me yes!

Chorus: Because my heart is your heart, and you're a part of me.
           Every moment's a brand new start, because our love was meant to be.

Vs3:   Each time I look at you, I realize it's true.
        And every time I feel your touch, I thank the Lord so much!

MY PROM QUEEN

Jon and Camille's prom date
7/19/89-7/20/89

Something special began the moment we danced,

Left me sleepless nights, it wasn't by chance.

I closed my eyes, thought only of you.

I couldn't sleep, I knew it was true.

You captured my heart, it burned inside.

Images of you, my mind couldn't hide.

The kiss of your lips, a gentle surprise;

I held you close, we said our goodbyes.

Something started, somehow, somewhere, a special moment began.

I couldn't sleep at all that night, a special moment began.

I called you up, you answered the phone.

I needed to see you, I felt alone.

I wanted to be more than just your friend.

I knew my feelings would never end.

It took some time to give you my heart.

I took it slow, but I knew from the start.

I was caring for you, my feelings were deep.

I gave you my love, it's a promise I'll keep.

Something started, somehow, somewhere, a special moment began.

You gave me love that I feel now, a special moment began.

So always remember you're a part of me,

'Cause our special moment will always be!

Camille and I were married on June 6, 1992! Our son, Brandon, was born on May 3, 1994. Our life got a little busy, and my pen remained silent. On our five-year anniversary, I received some inspiration before we celebrated that great day.

5 YEARS OF MARRIAGE!

Year one is for romance; it's doing little things,
Like walking through a park, and kissing under a tree,
Or watching a funny movie with you snuggling next to me.
So walk up to the VCR and push the button play.
Sit down on our loveseat and enjoy our special day.

Year two is just remembering the promise I made to you.
It could be a little gift, something you love to do.
It's hidden in the kitchen, in one of the cabinets.
It won't take long for you to find, and you'll love what you will get!

Year three calls for a symbol of our love,
Something to remind you, your beauty's from above.
Perhaps a flower or two, maybe a bouquet,
Because you need to know, your love is A-OK!
Soft, like a flower petal, your skin feels next to mine.
Each time that I touch you is like the very first time.
Your fragrance is so tantalizing that I'm finally realizing, my love's forever yours.

Year four deserves a token of love, given from the heart,
A gift you'll always cherish whenever we're apart.
Something when you look at it, it makes you think of me,
About how much you mean to me, and make me feel complete.

Year five deserves a dinner out, just the two of us,
And free babysitting, with someone whom we trust.
We'll sit in candlelight and savor every bite,
And stare into each other's eyes on this fiesta night.
We once ate dinner at this place, the night before we wed;
If you need help remembering, you'll look a little red.
C.M. (Carlos Murphy's) is its initials, the same as your maiden name (Camille Merritt).
That was your last clue, to solve this silly game.

Our son, Nicholas, was born on January 7, 1999. Once again, life got a little busy.
My pen remained silent.

3

Pets

MR. JULIAN
11/30/07
In memory of Julian, our faithful first dog

We celebrated one year of marriage away from our first home.
We traveled to the Julian Lodge. We shopped and brought a dog home.
He was a yellow retriever lab puppy, handsome, with giant paws.
He was lost and a little lucky, *FREE PUPPIES*, the sign 'twas.
His dark brown eyes looking at you, so sad,
As if to say, pick me, you won't be mad.
Fourteen sweet years together, playing and having fun,
Eating popcorn and watching movies, and napping in the sun.
Shaking hands and giving kisses, taking walks together down the street.
You licking up what my vacuum misses, enjoying an occasional treat.
We love you, puppy boy, Mr. Julian. You brought us so much joy.
Playing hide and seek with the children, we love you, good ol' boy!

ZOEY
5/13/15

Zoey is our family cat; she used to be a stray.
She slowly came into our lives as we fed her day by day.
We have loved her and enjoyed her, and now she is not alone.
Each day Zoey comes running back to me; she thinks I will feed her anyway.
At night she is busy on her own, doing her own thing.
But each morning, Zoey awakes me and curls up beside me to say:
"Oh Master, will you feed me?" I think is what she would say.
My son, Nick, told me to write this story about her; she is his kitty too.
And even though life is crazy at times,
We don't mind living in a zoo!

OUR BEAGLE LUCY
5/16/15

Lucy Magoosey Pudding and Pie, you are such a sweetheart to me;

Sometimes you just make me cry!

Those sad, dark brown eyes of yours, looking straight up at me.

Your little paws opening up all of our doors; we love you, can't you see?

We will rub your belly any old day, even give you a little treat.

'Cause when we pet you, the world is OK,

And all of us think that that is pretty neat.

RUBY
9/29/19

Ruby was a rescue dog; her hip was on the mend.

Camille was in remission and needed a new friend.

We needed something special, to help us lift our moods.

We prayed and we prayed; finally, God sent us Rubes!

She loves to snuggle with you, on a couch or chair.

Wherever you go in the house, Ruby will be there.

Give her a toy, or she might pick up your shoe.

She's always looking for something yummy to chew.

Football is Ruby's favorite toy to catch.

Thank you, Lord, this dog's a perfect match!

4

Reflections

AMAZING GRACE
In memory of Uncle Steve

Have you ever listened to a song that holds a very special place in your heart, and, all at once, it takes you back in time? For some people, it might be a song played on their wedding day or at a happy occasion in their life. For others, it might be a song played during a very sad occasion. This song happens to hold both places in my heart. This song reminds me of my Savior's love for me. It also gives me hope for tomorrow. And every time that I hear it, my thoughts flood my mind with memories of a single day in my life. This song is "Amazing Grace."

It was Sunday morning, December 2, 2007. Our family packed into our little Dodge Caravan, but, instead of going straight to church, we made a three-hour drive to visit our Uncle Steve. Steve had been in hospice, suffering from pancreatic cancer. This would be a trip to say goodbye. One of our sons, Brandon, had decided that he would stay home. He wanted to remember Uncle Steve the way that he always was: big and tall, strong and loud, with his booming voice, bushy beard, and fabulous smile. He was a very accepting man, the kind of guy that always made you feel better to be around. Nicholas, our younger son, accompanied us on the trip, along with Jim, Gloria, and Bethany. Virginia , or "Grammie" to most of us, also made the trek. She was Mom to Jim, Gregory, Steve, and Carl. She gladly enjoyed a nice drive away from her assisted living quarters. Her mind and health had been in decline, but she added a sense of innocence to our sobering, long drive.

We had arrived. After hugs and a few tears with Steve's family, we slowly entered into his room. Barely recognizable, we saw the shell of the man that we all loved. As we circled his bed, Steve's eyes caught a glimpse of his mother. He called out to her: "Mom! Mom!" And he insisted that she sit on the bed next to him. Although it was difficult for Virginia to get around, she somehow managed to crawl into bed next to her son.

I'm not sure if someone had asked me to pray, but suddenly I knew just what to do. "It's Sunday morning and we all missed church, so let's have church here. Why don't we sing Amazing Grace?" We choked back the tears and sang through the first line of that great hymn of the faith, our hearts not willing to continue. In the silence, we all heard Steve's whispering voice, "'Twas Grace." We had to go on. The second line was even harder than the first! However, thanks be to God, we all found strength to finish the song.

"'Twas grace that taught my heart to fear, and grace my fears relieved. How precious did that grace appear, the hour I first believed?" Steve's body was failing him, but his spirit was still strong. I could see Jesus in his eyes. Steve had reminded us that the only thing we can take with us, when we leave this place, is the grace of God. Steve knew it and he believed it! Ephesians 2:8: "For by grace you have been saved through faith, and that not of yourselves, it is the gift of God, not of works, lest anyone should boast." Did you catch that? Grace is a gift from God. Jesus is the gift, and Jesus is grace. John 3:16: "For God so loved the world that He gave His only begotten Son, that whoever believes in Him should not perish but have everlasting life." Steve believed, and right now he is enjoying eternity with Christ! Will you believe? Will you receive the gift?

You might say, "Why the sad story? What's this got to do with Christmas?" I would say, "Everything." You see, I was at church the other Sunday. We sang Christmas hymns and songs, all except for one. You have probably guessed that that one song was "Amazing Grace." You would be correct. As we sang it, I thought about my Savior's love for me and my hope for tomorrow. I thought about Steve whispering, "'Twas Grace." I also wondered why this song was picked along with all the other cheerful Christmas songs. Then I realized Amazing Grace has everything to do with Christmas. Amazing Grace is the reason why Jesus was born, why He came, and who He came to die for. "Amazing grace, how sweet the sound, that saved a wretch like me. I once was lost, but now am found. Was blind, but now I see."

CARL

6/3/15
Dedicated to Carl

Carl is my prayer partner. We started praying together before Brandon was born, approximately 21 years ago. We pray once a week for fifteen minutes, on the phone, usually on Wednesday mornings, at 7 AM. It all started when Jeremiah came to LMCC, our church. Jeremiah started the men's E-Teams. "E" stands for Encouragement! Teams of three men were assigned by Jeremiah to have a conference phone call to pray, once a week. Chris was our other prayer partner for the first year or so. Chris has since moved on, but Carl has been my faithful prayer partner ever since we first started. We have prayed over our struggles, our families, our nation, our missionaries, our church body, and maybe even some of you! There is a lot that you can pray for in 15 minutes! The time flies by quickly when you are in prayer with a brother.

Now I will admit that I do not always want to pray, and sometimes I even forget that Carl is going to be calling until the phone rings. Prayer is powerful! How can you pray without admitting your sins? When you pray, God unlocks the door to your heart and turns your heart of stone into a heart of flesh. Before long, you have gotten back on track with your Lord.

I am thankful for my prayer partner, Carl. I am thankful for Carl, my friend. We have seen God answer many prayers together over the years! Some prayers He has not answered. Some prayers He may answer someday, in His time. We do not stop praying these prayers, for these prayers are the most precious prayers near and dear to our hearts. Isn't it interesting that our most precious prayers can sometimes be the ones that God has not yet answered? Why is this? These prayers usually are for our loved ones. All I know is that God wants us to keep praying for them. Do we trust in Him? If God says no, will we continue to trust in Him? Will we just simply pray and humble ourselves before Him? Remember the story of the man whose son was demon-possessed, who said Jesus could heal his son if He wanted to? The man humbled himself before Jesus, seeking the truth. He simply said, "Lord, I do believe, please help me with my unbelief." Give it a try, my friend. The Father is waiting to hear from you! Jeremiah 29:11-13

Mailman Jon

MY DAD GOES TO CHURCH
4/25/18
Dedicated to my dad, Dan

Some of the earliest memories of my dad include him taking my mom and us kids to church every Sunday. My dad worked hard during the week. He wore a suit to work every day and carried a briefcase. His job was important! But on Saturdays, my dad would wear a white t-shirt and jeans. He would fix things and work on projects around the house. I usually hung out in the big tree in our front yard or played with Legos on the front porch while Dad worked in the garage. Sometimes, I would be sent to Dad "to help." He had Christian radio, KECR, on all day long while he worked. I would hear Bible stories, trivia, and great hymns of the faith. I enjoyed working alongside my dad and discussing the Bible and questions a young boy has in life.

Even though my dad worked so hard during the week, he still got up early on Sunday mornings. I could hear him shaving and getting cleaned up. I'd watch him tying his tie and putting his best suit on. I'd smell the cologne he had splashed on his face. This really struck me as a young boy - so much so that, at around six years of age, I begged my mom to get me a suit like Dad's that I could wear to church. Mom took me to Sears or JC Penney's and helped me pick out a blue, three-piece, striped suit with a clip-on tie! I was so proud to wear that suit to church, every Sunday, as long as it fit. Old folks would comment on how sharp I looked. Usually, at some point during the sermon, my coat would come off and I would lay my head in my dad's lap. Dad would rub my back, and, boy, did that really feel good! It is no small secret that the Hyatt family loves to rub backs!

As I grew older, the little suit became smaller and no longer fit. No problem. One of the benefits of having two older brothers is getting their old suits and ties. I always had a few suits and a wide assortment of "real" ties, which my dad taught me how to tie. I realize now, as a father myself, wanting that first little suit was just me wanting to be like my dad. Today, as times have changed, our suits do not come out of the closet as often as they used to, but you can count on Dad and all his grown children - Danny, Tim, Robin, and Jon - still getting ready for church. Dad still waits for Mom to get ready and lock up the house. He opens the car door for her. I need to remember to do that one more. Thank you, Dad, for teaching me how to love and live like Jesus!

JESUS, 42 – SATAN, 0

Dedicated to my son, Nicholas

Sunday morning, my heart flooded with anticipation, hopes, and some fears of what our worship service would bring. It was Youth Sunday and our youngest son, Nick, was to be a part of the team on stage! But suddenly, Nick had been thrust into the starting rotation and had taken on not only lead guitar but also lead vocals as the worship leader! You see, Brian, our Worship Pastor, had recently lost his voice and had asked Nick to step into his shoes and lead the team. Brian would support Nick while playing the drums. Three students, Haley and Trinity on vocals, tambourine, and egg shaker, along with Elijah on djembe, completed the team, with regulars Scott on bass and Rosanna on keyboards.

With each song I felt joy like I had never experienced. You see, it was my first time seeing my son in action leading worship. Nick has been faithfully leading the high school youth group on Friday nights in worship at our church. He also has led worship at God's Extended Hand, a homeless outreach in downtown San Diego which our church supports.

But as we worshiped Sunday, I asked myself if I felt proud of my son. I decided what I really felt was joy worshiping God with my son and the church body! With each new song, I felt elation as if my son, Nicholas, had just scored a touchdown for Jesus! We finished that service after six songs and touchdowns for Jesus, arms raised in triumph, hands clapping praise for God, and even a few tears of joy to celebrate His victory!

Starbucks was on the menu next. Dad and son would discuss the events and wonders of the day. Today I was reminded that there really is no greater joy than for a man to see his son walking with our Lord! Psalm 127:3-5, Proverbs 23:24-25.

CHARGERS LAMENTATIONS

10/3/16

Dedicated to the Chargers, who eventually left San Diego

Dear Pastor Nathan,

The words of one solitary, lonely Chargers fan: Meaningless, meaningless, says the Chargers fan. Another season wasting away, another blown lead wasted! I said in my heart, what is new this season under the sun? A few new players, but with the same result: unable to finish games, the laughingstock of the NFL. There is a time to weep and a time to cheer, a time to blow leads and a time to win. Unfortunately, for the Chargers fan, too many times he mourns. Perhaps new coaches, players, a new stadium, or even a new owner or general manager could reverse what has already been and what forever will be? No, I said in my heart. This is our lot in San Diego, millions of dollars wasted on another losing season. Then I remembered another alternative. How about root for the other team? No, my heart says. Why don't you change the channel? Better yet, you pathetic loser and exasperated fan: turn off the TV, find some joy in something else in life, enjoy your family and friends, rest for your mind and soul. Remember that whatever happens in this life, Jesus saves. Jesus has conquered death, and you are on the winning side!

Have a great week, Pastor!

Jon :-)

A CALL TO GIVE   3/13/19

As a young boy, around nine or ten years of age, I heard my first sermon on giving to the Lord. It was at a Sunday night service, during which there was no Junior Church and children stayed upstairs with their parents, that the man spoke of giving to the Lord. How much money should I give? How much money does God need? These questions stirred within my head. As the man prayed for the offering, I can still remember looking into my wallet, which contained $9. I could give 1- 3 dollars, and that would be fine, but suddenly, I felt inside my heart that God wanted more. That night, I ended up giving everything my wallet contained ($9). This was a lot of money for a kid back in 1979.

Today, almost 40 years later, I was reminded of that day during our pastor's sermon on giving. I believe that when I was a child, I finally understood that God wanted my whole heart. When I gave everything to Him, I was placing my trust completely in Him and giving Him my whole heart. God changed my heart that night. I consistently have given to Him over the course of my childhood and through adulthood. In return, God has continued to supply for my needs and to provide me with the resources to give back to Him. Am I a rich man? No, not by the world's standards. However, in God's economy, I have gained Christ!

2 Corinthians 8:9: "For you know the grace of our Lord Jesus Christ, that though He was rich, yet for your sakes He became poor, that you through His poverty might become rich."

Dedicated to my Uncle Jack

When I was a young boy, 10-12 years of age, I saved and saved my hard-earned money from mowing lawns so I could buy an Atari system. I can remember playing hours and hours, trying to master Space Invaders. I only had a few games because the new games cost almost as much ($50) as a new Atari ($100). My mom had a brother named Jack, named after their dad. To me he was simply known as "Uncle Jack." Uncle Jack somehow knew someone who worked for Atari. He sent me this funky little contraption that was inserted where the games would be put in. The games came on little chips that I would put into the contraption and worked perfectly just like a new game would. I can remember writing my Uncle Jack and requesting my wish list. I would buy each game for $2 apiece (far cheaper than $50!). Before I knew it, I had over 50 Atari games. Needless to say, I became very popular on our street. Missile Command, River Raid, Frogger, Pac Man, Pit Fall, Break Out, Galaxian, Golf, Pong, Tennis, Basketball, Football, Circus Atari, Dragon Slayer, to name a few. I used to have a big blue bean bag that I would lean on as I conquered the universe playing my games! I enjoyed corresponding with my uncle, and I always looked forward to our vacations with his family.

Family disputes separated our families over the years and I lost contact with my Uncle Jack, who recently passed away. An uncle can have a big impact on his nephew. Little things that uncles do can go a long way in making a nephew feel loved and accepted. Nephews can gain confidence in their own abilities when you invest just a little time in their lives.

Recently, I found a t-shirt at Target that says: Atari Entertainment Technologies. I still feel kind of "cool" when I wear that shirt. :-)

NATALIE'S TREASURE

Dedicated to Natalie
Natalie suffers gracefully from Potts, a chronic syndrome

"Consider it pure joy, my brothers, whenever you face trials of many kinds, because you know that the testing of your faith develops perseverance. Perseverance must finish its work so that you may be mature and complete, not lacking anything. Blessed is the man who perseveres under trial, because when he has stood the test, he will receive the crown of life that God has promised to those who love him." James 1:2-4 & 12

Natalie's treasure is her purity and joy. Her purity comes from Jesus, who calls her his child. She has been washed white in the blood of the Lamb. Natalie's joy comes from God, her Father in heaven. And not just joy, but pure joy, the joy that only God can provide.

I do not know Natalie very well, but I do know that she has faced trials of many kinds. Why do some of God's people have to suffer so much, we may ask? James states: "...that the testing of your faith develops perseverance." Purity, pure joy, and perseverance all belong to Natalie. These are a testimony to many people of her witness of Christ's work through her life. She keeps pressing on toward the goal of the prize, because perseverance must finish its work in her. Natalie is blessed, and Natalie is a blessing. One day she will receive a pure crown and be filled with complete joy. "God has promised it to those who love him."

THE STITCH IN TIME

Dedicated to my mother-in-law, Gloria

It was a cold, windy day delivering the mail. I was almost finished when my windbreaker got caught on a nail on a telephone pole. I was sad because this was my cherished "Star Performer" jacket that I had received several years ago. The post office gave it to me for being a great mailman. (This was back in the day when they had money to do stuff like this!) The windbreaker has my name embroidered on it with the slogan *Star Performer*. In fact, the embroidery was done by a company that my brother, Tim, works for!

I knew just what I had to do, so I brought my cherished windbreaker to church. I handed it to my mother-in-law, Gloria, and asked, "Can it be saved?" Gloria loves to sew! She helps make prayer quilts with the prayer quilt ministry at our church. These quilts are given to folks who are facing surgery or even death. Before they receive these quilts, people at the church tie knots and pray over their prayer requests. Gloria took my windbreaker home from church not knowing if it could be saved.

Last night I was at Gloria's house and she proudly handed me my windbreaker. She had fixed it! However, as she looked over it again for a final inspection, Gloria noticed that the stitching was pulling loose. She told me not to worry. "I can put a patch on this and double stitch it," she said. Before I left, my cherished windbreaker was fixed and ready to get back into service!

Coming home I thought about Gloria. Our family is like patches on a quilt. Sometimes we need to be stitched back together. We need someone who knows what material to use and how to thread it, someone who cares and wants to do the job right. Gloria has cared for many people over the years without complaining: Willa, Virginia, Jim, and all the rest of us too. She may not know it, but we depend on her a lot! And not just to fix my windbreaker or hem up my postal pants! We need her. She is our example of unconditional love that the Father has for us. God knows when we need fixing. When stitches come loose or patches get torn off, God knows, and God cares. Sometimes He fixes our problems and sometimes He says, "My grace is sufficient for you!"

Heavenly Father, I thank you for putting me into Gloria's life. I LOVE MY MA, GLORIA! I hope that YOU give her a great Mother's Day. Comfort her as her mother is with YOU now. Remind her, when she sees the stitches on the seam, just how much you love her.

Mailman Jon

Dedicated to my mom, Charlene

I am a reflection of my mom. Many of my emotions come from my mom. I must have gotten one of her ribs! :-) I have a heart for people around me. I love my family. I love to write! All of these came from my mother and more! When I look around my house I am reminded of my mom. I see furniture and belongings that used to be her cherished items. Now she has passed them along to my family to enjoy. My mom used to save and pay money so that I could go to camp. Now she helps pay for my kids to go to camp. My mom loves to bless her family. She plans parties and get-togethers for the family. She writes to prisoners who love Jesus. She sends grief packets to those who have suffered loss. My mom is there for me when I need someone to talk to. She listens to me and lifts my spirit. I love my mom! Did you know that I still call my mom when I am sick? I am 45 years old, but I still like to hear my mom's voice. She comforts me and makes me feel better. Animals care for their young when they are little. A good mother always cares for her children - even when they have kids of their own! My mom cares for me. If I need a hug, she won't refuse me. When I blow it, she forgives me. I'm her child. She is my mom.

I still remember getting the house all cleaned up for my mom. I was probably about 16 years old. My mom was coming home from the hospital. She had had a close call and had come out of surgery. I polished and vacuumed everything in the house. I knew that my mom loves a clean house, and I wanted it to be special for her when she came home. As she was coming out of the car and being helped up the stairs to our house, I raced and found a record to play for her. I think it was from *Out of Africa*, but I cannot be sure now. Anyways, the music was playing when she walked in the door. It was perfect! All of us kids were hugging our mom and thankful that she was home. Not to brag or boast, but I just had to show my mom the house. Even though she didn't feel well, she graciously walked around the house and thanked me for getting it ready for her.

I think one of the hardest things for a son to see is his mother cry. Their heart strings pull at our hearts too, but when our mothers smile and laugh, we rejoice with them. There is a bond between a mother and her child that can never be broken - especially if your mom loves Jesus, like my mom does.

Father, thank you for giving me my mom! She gave birth to me. I was supposed to be the gift for her. My mom is a gift that you gave to me. Help me not to take her for granted. Help me to remember her, not just on Mother's Day. Jesus, I know that you loved your mother too. You wanted to make sure that she was taken care of when you left this earth. Mary watched you die for all mankind. How could she do it? Mary knew that her Son was going to rise again the third day! God entrusted her with His one and only Son.

Mom, words simply cannot express and give justice to my love for you. So for now I will simply say the words, "Happy Mother's Day, Mom."

I LOVE YOU!!!

Jonathan

GOD BLESS COSTCO

Dear Ginnie- Publisher, and Tim-Editor, of *The Costco Connection*:

I just simply love Costco! My family has always told me that I should write to *The Costco Connection* and share all of my Costco adventures! Well, I do have many stories to share. When I shop at Costco, I remember that I am an American! As I sip my mocha freeze, I enjoy exploring each and every aisle of the store. The employees are like family to me, and they greet me each and every time that I enter and exit the doors! The Kirkland products have been a lifesaver to our family during these hard economic times. The Costco food court has provided many high-quality and inexpensive meals for my family - and me too! I often joke with my family that when I retire someday, I will go and work for Costco in some kind of capacity. Maybe I'll be a greeter or push carts or even just sample mocha freezes across America! I love Costco! I thank God for Costco! God bless Costco and God bless the USA!!! Below is a song I was inspired to write about Costco.

Sincerely,
Jonathan Hyatt, member of Costco Wholesale, La Mesa, CA 91941

Inspired by the song "God Bless the USA" by Lee Greenwood,

If tomorrow all the things were gone I worked for all my life,
And I had to start again with just my children and my wife,
I'd thank my God above to be living here today,
Because I can still shop at Costco, and they can't take that away!

And I'm proud to be a Costco member, where all the samples are still free.
And I won't forget the men and women who stock those shelves for me.
And I'd gladly stand up, next to you, and push my cart there today,
'Cause there ain't no doubt, I love Costco, God bless the USA!

From the lakes of Minnesota to the hills of Tennessee,
Across the plains of Texas, from sea to shiny sea;
From Detroit down to Houston, and New York to LA,
Well, there's a Costco in every major town, and it's time to stand and say:

That I'm proud to be a Costco member, where all the samples are still free.
And I won't forget the men and women who stock those shelves for me.
And I'd gladly stand up, next to you, and push my cart there today,
'Cause there ain't no doubt, I love Costco, God bless the USA!
No there ain't no doubt, I love Costco, God bless the USA!

God bless the USA!!!

MISSIONARIES
5/13/15

What is a missionary? Where does a missionary go?

A missionary tells people God's story. God tells him where He wants him to go.

Why does the missionary do this? Because, Child, lots of people need to know.

Will he ever come back to us? Will he stay far away?

God will direct his paths, Child. God will show him the way.

How does the missionary do this? Isn't it hard every day?

They do it, my child, for Jesus, because He was the first missionary in His day!

OUR TESTIMONY AND WITNESS
5/13/15

What is my testimony? What am I supposed to say? I never did anything worth talking about. What would I say today? My testimony is my story, little things that You are teaching me, things that I need to talk about, what You are doing in me. People always ask me every day: "How are you doing, Jon?" They say, "What's going on in your life right now, Jon? What do you have to say?" Will I ever tell them what God is teaching me? Do I hear His voice? Will I obey? I will tell them this: "Yes, Joanna, this is a wonderful day that the Lord has made!" Or, "Glenn, praise God for this beautiful day! God is doing amazing things! This was the best week of my life!" "Oh really? What happened?" they say. "What did He do? Tell us, Jon, for we really want to know!" I will respond: "Well, God is teaching me many things, my friends. I have many stories of just how He is helping me to grow. How much time do you guys have to listen to what God has done in my life? Do you have time for just one story of mine? Hey, guys, why don't we go and grab a bite to eat, but only if you have a little bit of time. You see, Jesus is changing my life, my friends. Jesus is coming again. Jesus is with me every step of the way, because Jesus is my best friend!!!"

Jonathan Hyatt

THE TOAST

Dedicated to my son, Brandon, and my daughter-in-law, Itze

Wedding Day: December 20th, 2019

Brandon,

I can still remember the joy that I felt, walking your mom down the aisle as my wife. Today, you feel that joy. I can remember the joy that I felt when you were born. I became a dad and you became my son. One day, you will feel that joy. I remember teaching you how to ride a bike, our campouts, and your awards. I remember your first tackle and your first sack. They are written on this piece of scratch paper. I remember your graduation. Here is the ticket stub. These are mementos for a dad, great bookmarks for my Bible.

Brandon and Itze, I remember praying with Camille for Brandon's future wife. Today, God has answered our prayers through you, Itze! We have gained a daughter and we rejoice! 3 John 4 says, "I have no greater joy than to hear that my children walk in truth." Brandon and Itze, you have given Camille and me this joy. This is evident by everyone here today. We all rejoice in your marriage, we celebrate your love, and we will always remember this very special, joyful day!

Cheers!

On this beautiful wedding day, I felt so much joy witnessing the marriage of Brandon and Itze! I remember their faces glowing as they said their vows to each other. I remember the backdrop of the bay behind the wedding arch. It also was kind of cool seeing the Hyatt hotel, off in the distance; not that I happen to own it...

During the reception, time came for the groom and his mother, my wife Camille, to dance. Tears of joy streamed down my face as I watched my lovely bride dance with my son. Camille looked so very beautiful in her golden dress. Brandon smiled at his mom and gave her a couple of spins and twirls on the dance floor.

Praise! God did answer one small prayer of my heart. My wife, Camille, had a full head of hair for the wedding! Even her oncologist was surprised she still had hair! My first prayer had been for Camille to just feel well for the ceremony. Later, I went out on a limb and prayed to God that I thought it would be pretty cool if she could keep her hair as well. God does indeed have a sense of humor and He even has the hairs on our head numbered too.

Matthew 10:30-But the hairs on your head are all numbered.

5
Prayers

THE GREATEST COMPOSER
Inspired by Psalm 8

Vs 1a: "Oh Lord, our Lord, how majestic is your name in all the earth!"
           Who is the greatest writer, the greatest composer of all time?

Vss 3,4:   "When I consider your heavens, the work of your fingers, the moon and the stars,
           which you have set in place, what is man that you are mindful of him, the son of
           man that you care for him?"
           Why did you create us, oh Lord; why do you know us by name?

Vs 5:   "You have made him a little lower than the heavenly beings, and crowned him
           with glory and honor. You made him ruler over the works of your hands; you
           put everything under his feet."
           What did you give to me, Lord, under my feet? How can I rule all the works of
           your hands?

Vss 7,8:   "All the flocks and herds, and the beasts of the field, the birds of the air, and the
           fish of the sea."
           How can I respond to you, Lord, what do you want me to say?

Vs 9:   "Oh Lord, our Lord, how majestic is your name in all the earth!"
           I want to see you, oh Lord. Which way did you go?

Vss 1b, 2a: "You have set your glory above the heavens. From the lips of children and
           infants you have ordained praise."
           Why, oh my Lord, please open my eyes, why do you need so much praise?

Vs 2b: "Because of your enemies, to silence the foe and the avenger."

Numbers 22:31: "Then the Lord opened Balam's eyes, and he saw the angel of the Lord
           standing in the road with his sword drawn. So he bowed low and fell facedown."

GLORY TO GOD!   5/15

Lord, please give me a pure, gentle heart like Stephen, courage and strength like
Paul, wisdom and discernment like John, and a repentant heart like Peter, your Rock.

Thank you, God, for watching over me. I am not alone. You give me strength to
make it today.

Thank you for sending Gloria to help me today. I love your righteous right hand!

Isaiah 41:10, "So do not fear, for I am with you; do not be dismayed, for I am your God. I
will strengthen you and help you; I will uphold you with my righteous right hand."

Lord, please give me your wisdom to understand your knowledge. Be my counselor and give me the mind of Christ through your Holy Spirit. All I have to offer you is my heart that believes and trusts completely in you and your Son!

Romans 11:33-36, "Oh the depth of the riches of the wisdom and knowledge of God! How unsearchable his judgments, and his paths beyond tracing out! Who has known the mind of the Lord? Or who has been his counselor? Who has ever given to God, that God should repay him? For from him and through him and to him are all things. To him be the glory forever! Amen."

TRUE PEACE
9/26/16

Lord, please help me to listen when other people share.
Help me to let them know just how much I really care.
Their burdens are sometimes very heavy, Lord, but they are not for me to bear.
Lord, please remind me daily to offer them up to you in prayer.
It is easy to weep, it is easy to despair,
When my heart so aches for others to know Jesus is really there!
He offers the solution; it's called Amazing Grace.
God's word will penetrate your heart, change your countenance, change your face.
Rest for the weary soul, my child, please just call upon His name.
Place your hope in the Son of God; you will never be the same!
Life will still be a struggle, but you will never be alone,
Because Jesus will guide you through it when you place Him upon the throne.
Christian brothers He will send to encourage you, to remind you of His Grace.
So let your light shine before men; take up courage and finish the race.

God bless you, my friend, and I will see you Sunday!

Jon

THE DROUGHT
5/5/15

Oh righteous Father, the land here is very dry. You have withheld your rain from this land. You have withheld your showers of blessings. Will you send us your rain upon this dry and weary land once again, oh righteous Father? Will you send us your showers of blessings? Yes, our land is very wicked, oh righteous Father. Yes, our leaders have turned their backs away from you, oh righteous Father. Oh Lord, but you did send your rain in the days of your prophet Elijah. You did send your rain in the days of the wicked King Ahab. I am not a prophet, oh my righteous Father, but please help me to look for the little cloud in the sky. Please send us your rain again. Shower us with your blessings. I will tell all that you have sent the rain! I will sing and proclaim, "There shall be showers of blessing!"

There Shall Be Showers of Blessing
By Daniel W. Whittle, 1840-1901, and James McGranahan, 1840-1907
A great hymn of our faith

There shall be showers of blessing.
This is the promise of love.
There shall be seasons refreshing,
Sent from the Savior above.
There shall be showers of blessing,
Precious reviving again,
Over the hills and the valleys,
Sound of abundance of rain.
There shall be showers of blessing;
Send them upon us, O Lord.
Grant to us now a refreshing,
Come and now honor Thy Word.
There shall be showers of blessing,
Oh that today they might fall,
Now as to God we're confessing,
Now as on Jesus we call!
Showers of blessing,
Showers of blessing we need;
Mercy-drops round us are falling,
But for the showers we plead.

In 2015, California had been experiencing a severe drought. A few days after praying this prayer, I went to the National Day of Prayer at Shadow Mountain Community Church. Men joined me in prayer. God sent the rain!

THE WALK   10/3/18
Dedicated to my dear customers, Don and Deborah

He always smiles and he always waves. He shows up almost every day. Step by step he walks, making his rounds. He knows where he is going while he performs his duty. Some people know him as mailman, but many others know him by name. In fact, Mailman Jon, or Jonathan, knows most of them by name, too.

The job always gets done underneath the sun, but through the days and years together, a bond and a friendship has blossomed. We ask questions about each other or we may joke about the day, but when things go bad and the times get hard, you just might see us pray. What would you think if you drove by? That mailman is praying with that person; their heads are bowed down. What is going on? Is that even legal, you may ask?

Prayer is very powerful; and yes, people may notice you doing it. But for every prayer that you see, imagine the thousands of prayers which you don't. These are the prayers people pray for me and I pray for them - some silent prayers, some out loud. Every step that I take I remember His presence, for He goes with me along my route.

Jesus Christ, my Lord and my Savior, my Friend and my God, goes with me down every road. His Spirit dwells within my heart, and I know He has been there right from the very start.

Sometimes the path is hard on the road marked with suffering. The days may seem long and the finish line is out of sight. But I know that He is still there, waiting for me to remember Him, waiting for me to pray. "Jesus, help me through this mess; could you please help me through this day? In this trial, Lord, remind me of Your goodness; remind me You are the Way. And thank You, Lord, for reminding me: today's the day to pray!"

By Mailman Jon

COLOSSIANS 4:2-6   5/29/15

"Devote yourselves to prayer, being watchful and thankful. And pray for us, too, that God may open a door for our message, so that we may proclaim the mystery of Christ, for which I am in chains. Pray that I may proclaim it clearly, as I should. Be wise in the way you act toward outsiders; make the most of every opportunity. Let your conversation be always full of grace, seasoned with salt, so that you may know how to answer everyone."

DEVOTE: To consecrate or dedicate; to set apart for the Lord.

Oh righteous Father, make me watchful and thankful today, watching for your return and thankful that you have redeemed me. Open doors for my friends to share the good news. Speak clearly through your servants and give us wisdom. Always lead and direct our conversations with others about your grace; too much or too little salt can spoil your message. May your Holy Spirit help us to know how to answer everyone.

In Jesus' Name, Amen.

HEBREWS 4:12-13
6/1/15

"For the word of God is living and active, sharper than any double edged sword, it penetrates even to dividing soul and spirit, joints and marrow; it judges the thoughts and attitudes of the heart. Nothing in all creation is hidden from God's sight. Everything is uncovered and laid bare before the eyes of him to whom we must give account."

Lord, may your word penetrate Gregg's soul, spirit, joints, and marrow. May your Holy Spirit turn his heart of stone to a heart of flesh. May Gregg completely repent and come clean before you, oh my God.

JAMES 2:13

"Because judgment without mercy will be shown to anyone unmerciful. Mercy triumphs over judgment."

PROVERBS 3:3-4

"Let love and faithfulness never leave you; bind them around your neck, write them on the tablet of your heart. Then you will win favor and a good name in the sight of God and man."

Oh Father, thank you for your unconditional mercy to me! Make me into a merciful man, full of love and faithfulness. You have saved me when I deserved to go to Hell. Oh merciful Father, you have triumphed over my sin. Write your name upon my heart, show me your favor today, and give me a good name in the sight of God and man.

PRAYER FOR PETE'S MOM, LIZ
7/3/15
Titus 2:11-13, 3:5

"For the grace of God that brings salvation has appeared to all men. It teaches us to say 'no' to ungodliness and worldly passions, and to live self-controlled, upright and godly lives in this present age, while we wait for the blessed hope - the glorious appearing of our great God and Savior, Jesus Christ."

"He saved us, not because of righteous things we have done, but because of his mercy. He saved us through the washing of rebirth and renewal by the Holy Spirit."

God, may you save Liz because of your mercy! May she realize it all comes from you, through your Son, Jesus Christ. (My prayer for Pete and family today, as Pete's mom, Liz, is near the end of her life.) God answered this prayer!!! 9/15/15

"JESUS IS COMING AGAIN"
9/3/15

I thought of the chorus to this hymn today as I delivered my route. Keith, our Awana Commander, had spoken of being watchful and in prayer for Jesus' return. When this world is in chaos, we can rest assured, Jesus will come again. We can watch and look for His return.

Matthew 24:42

"Therefore keep watch, because you do not know on what day your Lord will come."

Matthew 24:44

"So you also must be ready, because the Son of Man will come at an hour when you do not expect him."

Matthew 25:13

"Therefore keep watch, because you do not know the day or the hour."

Mark 13:37

"What I say to you, I say to everyone: watch!"

JESUS IS COMING AGAIN
(Hymn Chorus)

Coming again, coming again

Maybe morning and maybe noon

Maybe evening and maybe soon

Coming again, coming again

Oh, what a wonderful day it will be

Jesus is coming again!

ARE MAILMEN IN HEAVEN?
7/22/16

Dear God,

Are mailmen in heaven? I know that you already have angels to deliver your messages, but I hope that I can help out, too, every now and then. You see, maybe I could deliver invitations to the Marriage Feast of the Lamb, walking along the streets of gold. Or, maybe I could carry a few gift baskets of fruit, nonperishable, of course, from the Tree of Life, along with their healing leaves and deliver them to someone's mansion in heaven. I could pass out bulletins for the worship service, every day forever, delivering the Good News to every tongue, tribe, and nation, saying, "Hey, guys, Jesus paid it all!!!" No more junk mail, bills, or condolence cards. I know that I won't ever get tired or hot. I probably won't even ever break a sweat. I also know that I will never thirst again. No more packed lunches or cold drinks to prepare. No more uniforms to wash or to wear. I will be dressed only in your fine, white, clean linen.

Lord, I promise not to deliver any bills, ever again, because you already paid for them all! I'm sure that there are lots of great routes in the New Jerusalem. I do prefer a walking route. However, a mounted route might be kind of fun; Pony Express was the way we used to get things done. I'll leave the Air Mail up to the angels, to spread their glad tidings of joy. What do you say, God?

Please keep me posted.

Mailman Jon

PSALM 4:4 & 8, 1 PETER 5:6-7

"In your anger do not sin; when you are on your beds, search your hearts and be silent."

"I will lie down and sleep in peace, for you alone, O Lord, make me dwell in safety."

Dear God, may I go to bed with a clean conscience and a pure heart and sleep in silence. I will lie down in peace and stay asleep, because you have saved me and you alone are my Protector. (6/30/16)

1 PETER 5:6-7

"Humble yourselves, therefore, under God's mighty hand, that He may lift you up in due time. Cast all your anxiety on him because He cares for you."

6

NOTES FROM A POSTMAN

POSTMASTER LETTER
March 29, 1991

Postmaster
7938 Broadway
Lemon Grove, CA 91945

Dear Postmaster:

My interview last Wednesday for the position of Carrier was very enlightening. I appreciate you taking the time to share the many opportunities that the United States Postal Service offers me.

Your description of these opportunities makes me even more certain I would like to become a postal employee. After hearing your explanation of the details of your operation, I feel confident I can make a significant contribution to your office. Thank you for telling me that I am headed in the right direction.

Thank you for your consideration.

Sincerely,

Jonathan Hyatt

Human Resources informed me that the Postmaster was trying to decide between hiring me or the other guy. This letter tipped the scales in my favor! My Business Communications class at Grossmont College helped me learn some invaluable interview skills, including the suggestion to send a thank you letter following the interview. I started my career as a USPS letter carrier approximately one week following my interview for the position.

PADRE DEBI
5/16/15
This story is dedicated to my dear customer and friend, Debi

Padre Debi is a remarkable lady. She knows all the players; she knows all their names.

Debi even knows the mailman's name, too!

She sits and waits for him almost every day.

A remarkable lady, you see, because she doesn't feel well most of the time.

Debi's lupus does not like to be kind.

A remarkable lady, because of who she is inside!

"How about a water, Jon, a cookie or some cake?"

Debi never hesitates.

And my friend Debi will always come get the mail,

Unless she is not awake!

I love you Debi!

Jonathan

SANTA'S MAILMAN
12/12/16
Dedicated to my dear friends and customers, Jere and Joy

When Santa gets too busy and starts to call out, "mush!"
The mailman just smiles and says, "Let me help you, what's the rush?"
"People are on the internet, ordering packages galore!"
"Hey Santa, come fill up my mail truck; I'll bring them to their door."
And not just on Christmas Day, but all throughout the year,
Santa's mailman makes his rounds, delivering good cheer!

CARL'S WOOD STUMP
5/16/15
This story is dedicated to Carl, a dear friend and customer on my route.

Carl has a wood stump in his front yard; he sits on it many days.

He waits for his mail and mailman, who takes a break there most days.

They like to talk about Jesus and what is happening in the world.

"What's happening in the neighborhood? Jonathan O'Reilly, O'Malley,
  O'Flanagan, Old Buddy of Mine?"

Carl indeed is my buddy; he's been my friend all of the way.

Sometimes I can't wait to see him, just to see what he has to say!

I love you, Carl!

Your buddy,

Jonathan

AT EASE, SOLDIER
5/4/15
For my dear customer and friend, Betty, in memory of her husband, Jim

Today I went to a military service at Miramar National Cemetery for one of my customers, Jim, who lived on my route. Jim loved Jesus and served his God, country, and family well. As the pastor spoke at the service, he shared the story of Jesus being presented to Simeon in the temple on the eighth day. As Simeon held Jesus in his arms he praised God, saying, "Sovereign Lord, as you have promised, you may now dismiss your servant in peace..." The pastor explained that Simeon being dismissed in peace is like the formal military practice of being "at ease, Soldier, dismissed." Like Simeon, Jim is now "at ease, Soldier, dismissed." Jim has entered into his peace and rest with our Lord Jesus, who now is holding Jim in His arms.

HOLEY SOCKS

5/2/15

Dedicated to my coworker, Jeff

Does God really care about holey socks? I had been noticing that my work socks were near the end of their life. My coworkers even laughed and scoffed at my holey socks, but I remained unscathed by their remarks. My holey socks were a badge of honor to me.

Over time, I realized that something did indeed need to be done, so I prayed a simple prayer. "Lord, please help these socks to make it until my next uniform allowance three months from now."

Several days later, I was making the rounds on my route. A retired mailman named Jeff drove by, and I waved to him as he passed by. Jeff had taught me all that I know about delivering the mail before he retired ten years ago. I replaced Jeff on my route. He was even the brother of the lovely Peggy from my church!

A few minutes later, Jeff returned on his bike with a plastic bag in his hands. "Jon, could you use some socks? Many of them are brand new or I only wore them once." "Sure!" I replied. Jeff rode his bike to my mail truck and placed the bag beside it. As I opened the bag, I said another simple prayer: "Lord, thank you for these socks."

I think that God was reminding me that "hey, Buddy, if I care about your socks, don't you think that I care about everything else in your life? Do you trust in me? I kept the Israelites' sandals from wearing out for 40 years. I healed the lame man's feet and even washed the disciples' feet. How beautiful are the feet of those who bring good news! And Jon, please don't worry. Remember Matthew 6:25-34? Your Heavenly Father knows that you need them. Seek Me first!"

Sometimes, God blesses our socks off! God didn't give me a new car because He knows that I didn't need one. My car is just fine. God gave me a bag of socks! :-)

GREGG'S GARAGE
5/31/15
Dedicated to Gregg , a dear friend and customer on my route

1 John 1:9 - "If we confess our sins, he is faithful and just and will forgive us our sins and purify us from all unrighteousness."

The first part of getting right with God is simply telling him that you are sorry and that you do need his help. God will help you through with all the rest, in His time. I wrote this poem while I was out from work, before I wrote Padre Debi. I am sending this only to you, Gregg, unless you tell me otherwise. I'm also sending it to myself, so that I can save it. Gregg, you are my friend, and I will see you the next time your garage is open, no matter what!!

Gregg's garage is a special place to me,

For when the door is open, I know that it is Gregg whom I will see.

Gregg is a brother of mine I've known for a long time.

We sit and talk about life, our families, and our wives, sometimes.

But Gregg's garage needs some redecorating; it needs some new pictures,
And the old wallpaper must come down.

But as for me now, I will keep my eyes looking straight, straight ahead.

I don't want any of Gregg's pictures to be stuck inside my head.

But when Gregg is ready, I will help this brother of mine.

Gregg will turn a new leaf, and we will have a great time!

We both will be looking forward, forward at Jesus, and all that He has done.

We will both be looking straight, straight at Jesus, and wanting to become more, and more, like God's Son!!!

Your friend and little buddy,

Jon

Camille and I visited Gregg and Debi at their new house in Arizona (3/6-3/7/19). We enjoyed hanging out together. Gregg and I also hung out in his new garage, and we had a great visit!

THE WIDOW'S PLIGHT
12/19/18
For Carol, my dear customer and friend, in loving memory of her husband, Lanny

She lost her dear husband, the love of her life.
No longer is she called his beautiful wife.
The holidays come and the holidays go.
Everyone seems to smile, but only a few people know.
She is heartbroken, she is lonely, she is in despair.
"Why did this have to happen to me? Life just isn't fair."
Everything around the house reminds her of her loss.
Only hope keeps her going on, only a greater love for His cross.
Jesus, be her husband; Jesus, be her guide.
Wash her daily in Your Word and comfort her inside.
Holy Spirit, intercede; we know not how to pray.
Remind this woman of Your love each and every day.
Merry Christmas, God our heavenly Father, may we walk by faith and not by sight.
Make us more like Jesus, and, Lord, please remember the widow's plight.

Revelation 21:2-4 – "Then I, John, saw the holy city, New Jerusalem, coming down out of heaven from God, prepared as a bride adorned for her husband. And I heard a loud voice from heaven saying, 'Behold, the tabernacle of God is with men, and He will dwell with them, and they shall be His people. God Himself will be with them and be their God. And God will wipe away every tear from their eyes; there shall be no more death, nor sorrow, nor crying. There shall be no more pain, for the former things have passed away.'"

THE HUMMINGBIRD
2/10/16

The front door on Ensenada Street had been left wide open. As I approached the door with the mail, my customer, Lauren, asked, "Jon, do you know how to get a bird out of your house?" The little red hummingbird peered at me through the glass window as I offered suggestions, such as shooing it out with a magazine. "I'm terrified of birds, Jon. And I really don't want to hurt it," Lauren said. I asked if I could be of assistance. Lauren brought me a red handkerchief. Slowly, I placed the cloth behind the hummingbird, against the window. I gently closed my hand, with no pressure applied to the bird. It kind of felt like catching a moth, but the bird, oh so tired, remained still. As I walked outside and down the porch, I opened my hand into the air. To our delight, the little hummingbird flew far away, free at last. No more glass in his way, just a lot of sky in sight!

PSALM 119:73 - "Your hands made me and formed me; give me understanding to learn your commands."

Below is the first story I wrote. I've decided to write these notes down when God reveals Himself to me through my travels delivering the mail. I like sending them out to folks to try to encourage them and remind them that God really cares for us! Please feel free to pass these stories along to your friends!

ABEL'S LITTLE NOTE
5/4/15
Dedicated to Abel and his Family

It was just another day for me delivering the mail on my route. I had about one hour of deliveries left when I opened the next mailbox on my route. I noticed the flag was up so I knew there was something to pick up. To my surprise, there was a small envelope inside that said, "To: Mailman, From Abel." Abel is a nice five- or six-year-old boy I know well. His family attends the Foursquare Church on my route. Abel often asks me if I want some water and brings me a water bottle. I noticed that there was a heart on the envelope as I opened it. Inside was Abel's little note that said, "Mailman, you are a good mailman." I smiled as I read the note, and I tucked it into my shirt pocket. Abel's little note of encouragement really made my day, and I showed it to my wife and boys when I got home. The next day I thought about why I am a good mailman. Instantly, I knew the answer. I love Jesus! The simple truth that Jesus loves me, and I love Jesus, makes me want to do everything for His glory. I also thought about God's goodness and how His Spirit helps me to be good. I could look up numerous scriptures to support this, but instead I have prepared a card to give to Abel that says, "Your thoughtfulness is a reflection of God's heart. Thank you for encouraging me. I try to be the best mailman because I love Jesus and Jesus loves me. Jesus loves you too! Love, Mailman Jon." :) Thanks for reading my little story about Abel's little note! Remember, God is good and Jesus loves you!!!

ABEL'S THREE CHRISTMAS GIFTS

Hello, my dear friends,

I hope that you all had a blessed Christmas and a Happy New Year! I wanted to give you an update on my little friend, Abel. Some of you may remember my story about Abel's little note, and how his kindness really inspired and encouraged me. This is off the cuff, so bear with me...

It was a few days before Christmas as I was making my rounds delivering cards, presents, and goodies. My dear little friend, Abel, a small boy around six years old, quietly approached me and said, "Merry Christmas, Mailman. This is for you." He stretched out his arm and handed me a Christmas card. Inside the card Abel's handwritten words said: "To Mailman. Thahk you for maiLin (some unreadable gibberish) mail. :)" I thanked Abel and shook his hand and wished him a Merry Christmas and I proceeded with my route.

The very next day, Abel ran up to me and said that he had a present for me. I was surprised this time around since he had already given me the card. The present was wrapped in tissue paper with plenty of tape on it. I unwrapped it at home. The gift was a small wooden cross ornament with an old piece of rope to hang it on the Christmas tree. Wow! I thought to myself. This is why we have Christmas! Jesus was born for this very reason. He came to earth to go to the cross. What a great reminder of God's gift to you and to me!

Well, it turns out that Abel wasn't done bearing his gifts just yet. As I passed by his house at the end of the day, Abel came running up to me and gave me a plate of cookies which his mother and he had made for me! What a reminder that Christmas is a season to celebrate and fellowship with others!

So Mailman Jon got three small gifts for Christmas from one little boy who loves Jesus. Now I can only wonder if Abel got the idea of giving three gifts from the wise men, who also gave little Jesus three gifts; but I think that his inspiration really came from God. God's gifts just keep on giving, and we cannot possibly keep them all to ourselves!

Mailman Jon

7
POEMS

MY RAINBOW
5/11/15

Genesis 9:13, "I have set My Rainbow in the clouds, and it will be the sign of the covenant between me and the earth."

My Rainbow is straight.
Man's rainbow is crooked.
I want to fix man. I can fix anything!
Man tries to be woman and woman tries to be man.
I want them to be like Me! Made in My image!
I long to restore them; I long to change their heart.
But, Child, you must be willing;
Otherwise, your life will fall apart.

1 Corinthians 6:9-11, "....and that is what some of you were. But you were washed, you were sanctified, you were justified in the name of the Lord Jesus Christ and by the Spirit of our God."

(This was my prayer for my beautiful friends. Jesus does not like what they do, but He still loves them!)

TIM
3/22/19
Dedicated to my brother, Tim

You taught me how to play Monopoly, Clue, and Risk.
We watched Perry Mason, and you knew every plot, turn, and twist.
I tried to make cool Lego creations;
My big brother's my motivation.
Two-handed back rubs, watching the clock.
Needed help finishing a puzzle? My brother Tim, he always taught.
We still hang out together and call from time to time.
A friend who sticks closer than a brother is very hard to find!

THE 10 COMMANDMENTS
11/29/16

God gave Moses the Ten Commandments, only God wrote with finger in stone.

Moses came down off that mountain; then he broke them when he got back home.

Up, up the mountain he climbed again. "God, please show me your face."

"You can see only my back today, until I send you my Grace."

He calls us to obey them, all of them one by one.

He turns our hearts from stone to flesh. He covers us with His Son.

Exodus 33:13 - "Now therefore, I pray, if I have found grace in Your sight, show me now Your way, that I may know You and that I may find grace in Your sight. And consider that this nation is Your people."

Exodus 33:17-22 - "So the Lord said to Moses, 'I will also do this thing that you have spoken; for you have found grace in My sight, and I know you by name.' And he said, 'Please, show me Your glory.' Then He said, 'I will make all My goodness pass before you, and I will proclaim the name of the Lord before you. I will be gracious, and I will have compassion.' But He said, 'You cannot see me, and live.' And the Lord said, 'Here is a place by Me, and you shall stand on the rock. So it shall be, while My glory passes by, that I will put you in the cleft of the rock, and I will cover you with My hand while I pass by. Then I will take away My hand, and you shall see My back; but My face shall not be seen.'"

THE GAME
8/11/19
Dedicated to my father-in-law, Jim

Playing "The Game" with Jim involves strategic planning and calculated moves.

My mind fills with possibilities as I gaze at the board.

I purchase my units: infantry, tanks, planes, and ships.

Destroying my opponent is my reward.

The world is at war, and only one can prevail.

So a roll of the dice will determine the outcome.

Battles are won and battles are lost each round.

Winning or losing, Jim and I have so much fun.

When victory is in our grasp or defeat seems inevitable,

The defeated one simply concedes the loss.

Pieces of the game go back to their beginning places,

A new game begins, and we find out who is boss!

PETE

8/13/19

Dedicated to Pete

One day after my world was shattered, you were there.

You reached out to me and I shared with you my fear.

Many days have passed, hills and valleys along the way,

Yet you remain faithful, praying for over one year.

Words of wisdom and words of hope you have spoken,

Pointing me up, to God's grace and His love.

Your gave us two small olive wooden crosses,

To hold and to carry, while looking above.

You taught me to STUDY and what each letter means:

To STAY close to God, while TEACHING others to do the same;

To UNDERSTAND God and to DIE to one's self;

Always YIELDING to God while trusting in Jesus' name.

"...bringing every thought into captivity to the obedience of Christ."

"Let us therefore come boldly to the throne of grace,

That we may obtain mercy and find grace to help in time of need."

Scripture and prayer provide us endurance to run the race!

"And let us not grow weary while doing good,

For in due season we shall reap if we do not lose heart."

Thank you, my friend, for investing your time in me!

"...Let us do good to all..." "Oh, let the Ancient Words impart!"

Scripture verses cited, which you shared with me: 2 Cor. 10:5, Heb. 4:16, Gal 6:9

Worship song: Ancient Words

DANNY
Dedicated to my brother, Dan

His name is Dan Jr., and he sports a fine mustache.

He's very good with money, and he always pays with cash.

He's a frequent flyer selling energy, crossing from state to state,

Always has his laptop handy, reading a good book while he waits.

He will talk with the waiter; he didn't vote for Ralph Nader.

He's a man of many talents, like Papa, in many ways.

If you've got a flat tire, or you need a hot wire, Uncle Dan will save the day!

Camp fire stories or past fishing glories, this man loves the great outdoors.

He loves solar panels and anything flannel, and napping on family floors,

If you need to confide, or somewhere to hide, do not do a Google search.

Happy birthday, Big Brother; you're unique - there's no other.

Now go eat some cake, for goodness' sake!

ROBIN
Dedicated to my sister, Robin

My dearest sister Robin,

You are loved beyond all measure.

The love you give out, others treasure.

A woman of God and a woman for God,

You pray in secret places, and heaven applauds!

Your tears are precious, an offering poured out of love;

Grounded in your hope, you fly high,

With the Spirit of the dove.

SANTA'S SURPRISE FOR CAMMIE
12/24/16
Dedicated to my lovely wife, Camille

Dear Cammie, my darling, you sweet little girl!

Such a kindhearted soul, with your beautiful curls.

Come now! Open my present, and open it quick!

And remember, nobody loves you like I do, St. Nick!

With all my love, and with my eight reindeers' paws,

Merry Christmas, my darling, from good ol' Santa Claus!

(Jon helped Santa write this!)

SNOWFLAKES
12/16
Dedicated to my lovely wife, Camille

When snowflakes anew are falling, filling mountainsides with their snow,

Christmas time is among us, warming our hearts, while the fireside glows.

Scented candles burning flicker, snowmen décor throughout the house;

Nativity sets with baby Jesus, each figurine taking their bows.

So, Merry Christmas, my darling, this snowman's heart melts for you,

For God blessed this merry gentleman

The very day that you said, "I do!"

BUGSY
5/31/19
Dedicated to my co-worker, James "Bugsy"

Bugsy was a letter carrier in Lemon Grove. He retired after 50-years combined federal service: six years in the military and 44 years with the USPS. This is a tribute to Bugsy, loosely based off of Charlie Daniels' classic, "The Devil Went Down to Georgia."

Well, the devil went down to Lemon Grove; it was hot as hell that day.

He challenged our best carrier, and Bugsy said, "What the hay."

The stakes were high if he lost, and he knew what would lie in store,

But Bugsy didn't back down; to him, it was just another war.

He sorted the mail in a flash and hurried out the door,

Jumped in his truck, and finished his route, coming back for even more!

Well, the devil was a huffing and a puffing, and his face was turning red,

But Bugsy just kept on going, no matter what the devil said.

Now, the devil bowed his head, because he knew that he was beat.

He even walked with his tail between his legs, and he laid his satchel at Bugsy's feet.

Bugsy said, "Keep your satchel, you devil, and if you ever come back here again,

I'm gonna tell you once, you son of a gun, I'm the best there's ever been."

PRISONER OF CHRIST
11/05/19
Dedicated to Ismael, a brother incarcerated by man and a prisoner of Christ

Ismael, my beloved brother and prisoner of Christ, you are blessed.

In your darkest moment, you cried out to God, in that moment you confessed.

"The Lord gives freedom to the prisoners, My grace is sufficient for you."

"For My strength is made perfect in weakness;" now you have much work to do.

Lord, "Bring my soul out of prison, that I may praise Your name."

Your freedom is in Christ; this is why He came.

Inside these walls you praise Him, each and every day,

"A true son in the faith," a worker unashamed.

"Let the groaning of the prisoner come before You," oh Lord,

"According to the greatness of Your power."

From heaven hear their prayers cry out,

Fulfill their joy in You, with each and every hour.

"For we are the fragrance of Christ among those who are being saved."

"And among those who are perishing," the aroma of the grave.

"Who shall bring a charge against God's elect? It is God who justifies."

"Who shall separate us from the love of Christ?" You prisoner of Christ, He will glorify.

Yes, my beloved brother, yes indeed, you are so truly blessed!

"Come to Me, all you who labor and are heavy laden, and I will give you rest."

Scripture cited: Psalm 146:7, 2 Corinthians 12:9, Psalm 142:7, 1 Timothy 1:2, 2 Timothy 2:15, Psalm 79:11, John 17:13, 2 Corinthians 2:15, Romans 8:33 & 35, and Matthew 12:28

8
GOD'S CRADLE OF LOVE

Psalm 139:13-14 - "For You formed my inward parts; You covered me in my mother's womb. I will praise You, for I am fearfully and wonderfully made."

Written by my mother, Charlene, this poem is dedicated to Jon and Camille's first child, who passed away on Valentine's Day, February 14, 1993, during a miscarriage. One day, we will meet our son, Jake, or our daughter, Katelyn Rose, in heaven. We will spend eternity getting to know each other.

God's Cradle of Love

Little one sent here only awhile,
You became part of our lives
And brought to us many a smile.
When your daddy knew about you,
He could hardly wait to share
With everyone the good news.
Your mommy in her sweet, quiet way
Pondered the many changes you'd bring
When she lovingly cared for you one day.
Many others were excited too.
A special place is reserved
In our hearts just for you.
We don't know why God took you away,
But we do know He loves us
And thought it best you not stay.
You're waiting for us in heaven above,
Listening to angels sing soft lullabies,
Gently rocking in God's cradle of love.
Our hearts will rest, knowing you're fine.
Trusting you to our Heavenly Father's care,
We await the day to be with you, for all time.

By my mother, Charlene
Dedicated to our "little one"
February 1993

9
MY SERMON

This is an outline for my personal Bible study on Abel. I never actually preached this message. However, Abel's blood, by faith, still speaks to us and points us to Christ, whose blood was the perfect sacrifice.

1. Matthew 23:35: Abel's righteous blood shed. Judgment next chapter is the sign of the end of the age. Matthew 23:22: Swears by the altar. Can you say that God is ticked off? Understatement!!

2. Luke 11:51: Part of the Six Woes. Luke 12:4-12: Do not worry, even if you are killed by man. God takes care of the sparrows!

3. 1 John 3:11-24: Love one another. Do not be like Cain (1 John 2:18-27); watch out for Antichrists - prepare! 1 John 3:2: God is greater than our hearts! Vs1: This is how we know that we belong to the truth, and how our hearts are at rest in His presence!

4. Jude 11: Cain is the anti-Abel, the sin and doom of godless men.

5. Hebrews 11:4: Abel by faith still speaks. Faith is being sure of what we hope for and cannot see! Abel was commended for this!

6. Hebrews 12:24: Jesus the mediator; new covenant: HIS BLOOD SPEAKS A BETTER WORD THAN ABEL'S! A warning against refusing God. Hebrews 12:14...

7. Genesis 4:2-9:25: The story of Abel and subject of Abel.

8. Genesis 8:20-22: Noah's sacrifice pleasing to God; no more curse on the ground.

9. Genesis 9:1-17: God's covenant with Noah; His demand of man being held accountable for shedding each other's blood, for we are made in the image of God, by God!

10. The rainbow is the sign of the covenant between God and the earth!

11. We all know what mockery man has made of the image/sign of the rainbow, right?

12. Man will be judged!

13. Jesus is coming!!

14. We must prepare our hearts!!!

15. Do not be surprised when this happens!!!! 1 John 2:18-27

Thank you, Father, for revealing Your Word to me!!!!!

10
BREAKDOWN

THANKS
8/11/15

Thanks for your prayers and support! My anxiety attack happened in the middle of May, and I missed around two weeks of work. I got some treatment and therapy going, both at Kaiser and from Pastor Nathan, Pete , Jeff , and my prayer partner, Carl . My family and the church family at LMCC have been very supportive through all of this. I have recently been cleared by my therapist. I am still taking some medication, but I hope to get weaned off of it when I see my psychiatrist in October. She is not ready to label me as manic-bipolar yet, based on my situation, age, and lack of past history. I'm keeping an open mind, and God has taught me a lot about grace. I'd like to share my story with you, so here it goes.

I was on vacation the week before my breakdown. I wanted to have a spiritual vacation/retreat. My quiet times with God had been wonderful and consistent for about a month. During my week off, I got less and less sleep as I started writing all the little stories and poems I felt God was putting on my heart. I wanted to weep with those who weep. I really felt close to God, but my wife, Camille, has said since then that it seemed like I was losing touch with reality a little bit. I had some stresses in my life, but nothing major, I thought...I went back to work on two hours' sleep and prayed that I could stay on top of the mountain. I started witnessing to customers and coworkers. I felt Jesus was coming back really soon. After working 11 hours, I couldn't sleep. I actually got up and was e-mailing Pastor Steve around 2 AM! This was probably a cry for help. I went back to work on one hour of sleep. I felt like I was carrying Jesus' cross as I delivered the mail. I found myself weeping uncontrollably. Verses and poems were going through my head like a tape recorder. I kept calling my parents, and, needless to say, they were very concerned. Finally, I felt like Jesus was saying, "Give that cross back to me. Now you know how it felt for me to carry it." I called my boss and told him I couldn't focus as I wept on the phone. My dad took me to Emergency, where I shared my faith with some patients and my doctor. The rest is history!

Romans 12:15 "Rejoice with those who rejoice, and weep with those who weep."

Philippians 4:6-8 "Be anxious for nothing, but in everything by prayer and supplication, with thanksgiving, let your requests be made known to God, and the peace of God, which surpasses all understanding, will guard your hearts and minds through Christ Jesus."

MANIC 4 JESUS!
5/13/15

I went to the ER, couldn't finish the day.

Jesus walked with me, and I carried His cross part of the way.

The burden was too great; I needed to get some help.

I couldn't weep anymore; I felt like a water spout.

Streams of mercy and prayers for the lost had been flooding my soul,

But I felt like I was digging myself into a hole.

My Christian customers helped me for a little while.

I told Jesus, "Lord, please help me to go another mile."

We walked a few miles, with that cross strapped on my back.

Than Jesus said it's my turn, your heart's already snapped.

We can't save them all in one day, but we certainly tried.

We witnessed to many; we even made some of them cry.

Nobody turned us away, Lord; our story got to go out.

I thought this was the moment, like Enoch, I'd go out.

He was so close to you, Jesus, I wouldn't have made it, only God knows,

But I know I need to get better, and I have a long, long way to go.

But I have friends, and I have brothers and sisters to help me to grow,

Courage to keep on pressing, along with wisdom for understanding,

Rest for my heartbroken soul for the lost, and rest for this weary mailman.

Psalm 42:5 "Why are you cast down, O my soul? And why are you disquieted within me? Hope in God, for I shall yet praise Him for the help of His countenance."

Psalm 42:11 "Why are you cast down, O my soul? And why are you disquieted within me? Hope in God; for I shall yet praise Him, the help of my countenance and my God."

KOOKOO!
5/14/15

Hi, My Friends,

I got the therapy ball rolling today and got some help. My lovely wife, Camille, is my manager now. She is managing my health. God did something beautiful today. There was a couple at SMCC. Adena was in a terrible car accident two years ago, accidentally going up the freeway off-ramp! She pulled through a miracle! Her husband, Daryll, lost his job and they had to move to Texas. They moved back here recently and met my parents for lunch. Adena and Daryll paid for the lunch and handed my dad an envelope. "We want to thank you for all that you did for us in our time of need," they said. "Please take this gift." My parents held onto the gift, wondering what to do with it. Maybe help a missionary or . . . ?

Today, my dad gave Camille the envelope from Adena and Daryll. Dad said, "This is for you, Son; we want to help you and Camille get through." I hugged my dad and wept before our Lord. I thanked God for Adena and Daryll, and I hope to meet them one day. I also hope that Kim and Dan can meet them too!!!

Dad and I watched an old Bible movie on Peter and Paul. Dad rubbed my back, and I took off Dad's shoes and rubbed his feet. I felt like Jesus was rubbing my back, and I think that my dad might have felt like Jesus was rubbing his feet too!

I felt so close to our Lord today, but I still know that I have a long way to go. I love you guys, my brothers and sisters. I know that you will not forsake me. Please feel free to drop by or give me a call. I will not be working for at least a few more weeks.

Love,
Jonathan

Ps: I don't go by Jon anymore. Today my new name is Jonathan.

1 Peter 5:7 "Casting all your cares upon Him, for He cares for you"

PETE'S COUNSEL   5/16/15

1. Write and meditate Scripture, my questions, and prayers.
2. God speaks to me through His Word.
3. I speak to myself through my thoughts.
4. Do not carry all of the body of Christ's burdens; this is Jesus' job.
5. Rest.
6. Take care of myself and family.
7. Give all my bags of burdens to Jesus!

Isaiah 55:12 "You will go out in joy and be led forth in peace; the mountains and hills will burst into song before you, and all the trees of the field will clap their hands."

MY MILESTONE
11/07/15

Today is a milestone of sorts for me. Since 5/12/15, I have been taking medication for my condition. My medication was cut in half for the last thirty days, and I have felt better, even though I am working more hours. Tonight is my first night without medication! Praise God! May God grant me many a peaceful nights' sleep and restore me!

My doctors have determined that I have a thyroid condition. This will dramatically change the course of my treatment! I am no longer considered possibly bipolar. No more antidepressant drugs, with all of their side effects, no more meeting with my therapist. Now I simply take one little thyroid pill each morning before breakfast!

Thank you, God, for getting me through these last five months! I am so grateful for my family and friends who have encouraged and supported me. You have been with me every step of the way, Lord. May You be glorified through my life!

Isaiah 57:15
"For this is what the high and lofty one says - he who lives forever, whose name is holy: I live in a high and holy place, but also with him who is contrite and lowly in spirit, to revive the spirit of the lowly and to revive the heart of the contrite."

Oh Blessed Father,
Highly exalted above all of the heavens! Who can compare with you? Who can attain your holiness and splendor? Your kingdom is not of this world, yet your Spirit lives within my heart. My heart is humble and lowly before you, oh my Lord. If I stood before you, I would fall on my face and my hands before you, like every other man who has ever seen you. Revive my spirit and revive my heart, oh my God. Make me like your Son and create in me a clean heart, and renew a right spirit within me.
Amen.

Psalm 51:10
"Create in me a pure heart, O God, and renew a steadfast spirit within me."

Psalm 51:17
"The sacrifices of God are a broken spirit; a broken and contrite heart, O God, you will not despise."

11

MY JOURNAL

For Christmas, on 12/23/15, my son Brandon presented me with my first official journal. Up until receiving this gift, my journaling was scattered on papers and an old composition notebook. Below are the words of Brandon which also are the first words written in my journal.

Dad,

I am giving this journal to you because I have seen great fruit come out of journaling myself. Use this journal to write down your prayers, what God is teaching you, your dreams, hopes, and fears. Just write anything down and know that God is reading it too. If you read Psalms, you will see that the entire book is King David's journal. I have found that God speaks to me through my pen as I write, and I'm sure you will find the same. Take this with you to church because it's a great way to take sermon notes and read back on them later the following weeks. God will bless you if you take the time to write to Him. As you start to fill this journal, read back at your old entries, and you will be able to remember what God had on your heart, seeing how He was at work in you the whole time. When you finish this journal you will have grown in so many ways, so don't wait to fill it!

Love,

Brandon

Today, one of my customers, Glenn, asked me what God has been teaching me about "my experience/breakdown" last year. I have spent the last few weeks reflecting on my highs and my lows. Although I felt extremely close to God and inspired to write poetry and pray deeply for others, I lost touch with reality. While I was doing godly things and good things, I began to be consumed with having a deep responsibility to love and encourage the body of Christ and the lost. My sleeping habits went out the window. I found myself, at multiple times throughout the night, praying, meditating, and writing my thoughts down.

On May 12, 2015, I tried to work on one hour of sleep, this after a brutal eleven-hour work day. I felt like I had weights on my legs as I prayed while delivering the mail. I shared my faith throughout the day, feeling that Jesus was coming back soon. Finally, unable to focus on my work responsibilities, I called my supervisor and told him I couldn't stop crying. He told me that was all he needed to hear and to bring the mail back, if I could do so safely. I called my parents, who met me at the post office. I had probably called them eight or nine times that morning, feeling that God wanted me to talk with Dr. David Jeremiah and share my feelings!

Before I called my boss, I felt like God spoke to my heart saying, "Let Me carry that cross; that is My job. Now you know just a little bit what it feels like..." I cried to God, "I am so sorry I failed you. I can't carry this cross any longer." Just a few hours earlier, I had prayed continuously, "Lord, help me to walk like Enoch walked, go an extra mile for you. I got to tell them about Jesus, he's the only way. I got to tell them about Jesus 'cause He's coming back today. People all around me are dying. They need someone to show them the way. I got to tell them about Jesus, because He might come back today." This was like a tape recording in my head, repeating over and over again. So, what did I learn, and what is God teaching me?

1. Give my burdens to God; let Him carry them. That is His job, not mine.
2. Love like Jesus loved.
3. Get rest. Heal. God doesn't stop working when I call it a day!
4. Pray Scripture. You sure can't go wrong praying God's words!
5. Write out my thoughts in my journal.
6. Listen to God.
7. Christ lives in me. Remember Christ lives in me!

Key hymn God put on my heart today: "Jesus Paid it All"

Key verse: John 3:16, "For God so loved the world that He gave His only begotten Son, that whoever believes in Him should not perish but have everlasting life."

Prayer: God, help me to so love the world, and to let them know just how much you really do love them and me.

Isaiah 42:5-9 "Thus says God the Lord, Who created the heavens and stretched them out, Who spread forth the earth and that which comes from it, Who gives breath to the people on it, and spirit to those who walk on it: 'I, the Lord, have called you into righteousness, and will hold Your hand; I will keep You and give You as a covenant to the people, as a light to the Gentiles, to open blind eyes, to bring prisoners from the prison, those who sit in darkness from the prison house. I am the Lord, that is My name; and My glory I will not give to another, nor My praise to carved images. Behold, the former things have come to pass, and new things I declare; before they spring forth I tell you of them.'"

2 Corinthians 5:17 "Therefore, if anyone is in Christ, he is a new creation; old things have passed away; behold, all things have become new."

Acts 17:24 "God, who made the world and everything in it, since He is Lord of heaven and earth, does not dwell in temples made with hands."

Revelation 21:5 "Then He who sat on the throne said, 'Behold, I make all things new.' And He said to me, 'Write, for these words are true and faithful.'"

5/6/16

I mailed a card to my Uncle Bruce, to encourage him. He is undergoing chemo for lymphoma. In the card, I mentioned that I pray for Bruce when I pass by Peter's house on my route. Peter had been battling cancer again, for over a year. I have been praying for Peter when I deliver his mail.

Today I had a package for Peter's wife, Daniela. They had just gotten bad news from their oncologist: no more chemo and six months to live! Daniela invited me in to visit Peter. As he was lying in his bed, I prayed for them: "Jesus, you make all things new" (Steven Curtis Chapman). Peter said that he would pray for Bruce and offered some advice on his chemo: "Put some lidocaine on the port or around it, to numb it, and put some cellophane over it before your treatments. This will numb the area…" I assured Peter that Bruce would also pray for him.

"God, help me to continue to pray for Peter, even though the doctors give him no hope…Holy Spirit, please utter prayers on behalf of Peter and Daniela, for me… Amen."

I found out today that my customer, Peter, passed away peacefully last Monday. I prayed for Peter and his wife Daniela whenever I passed by their house, making my rounds. On 5/6/16, I also began praying for Bruce and Debi's healing, whenever I passed by Peter's house. God chose to heal Bruce completely from cancer! God also chose to heal Peter from cancer, yet in a different way. Daniela shared that she prayed that Peter would be pain-free and see God in all of His glory. She shared with me that she asked God to show her somehow and increase her faith. (She had seen her mother suffer much before she died.) Peter did indeed know the Lord. I could see the pain in his face, in the photo of him, before he passed away. He was under morphine and unresponsive. The picture of Peter after he died shows a smile on his face! Daniela said that the smile remained on his face even when the coroner finally arrived. I was reminded of the song, "Your Presence Lord," by Hillsong. Peter is experiencing all of God's glory, face to face now! I will continue to pray for Daniela, for comfort and healing, from the loss of her dear husband of eight years. I also will continue to pray for Bruce and Debi's continued clean bill of health when I pass by Peter and Daniela's house. 1 Corinthians 13:12-13 says: "For now we see in a mirror dimly, but then face to face. Now I know in part, but then I shall know just as I also am known. And now abide faith, hope, love, these three, but the greatest of these is love."

CAMP
10/7/16 – 10/9/16

I volunteered as a Staff Aid at Pine Valley Bible Camp. My duties included lighting group fires at Fireside and Victory Circle, working the coffee bar in Shiloh, brewing 30 gallons of coffee, hot water for tea, and replenishing the drinking water. I also helped out at the basketball tournament. Andrew, was also a volunteer. He drove the shuttle golf cart, transporting campers and putting out my fires. We stayed in a portable trailer and enjoyed serving over 340 men!

This was the second time my friend Mike, asked me to volunteer. I really enjoyed serving. I also got to listen to a great speaker named Joe. Three hundred and forty men worshipped God, led by a group of brothers, from Clairemont Emmanuel, who led our worship services. The food was awesome, as always. Lastly, I enjoyed the 7 a.m. chapel service/prayer with the director of PVBC, Steve.

10/18/16

This morning, I cooked breakfast for Russ, Guy, Mike, and Carl. We had a great time fellowshipping. After we ate, we spent some time talking about contentment. Are we content? I shared my testimony of financial loss. We talked about the Apostle Paul's attitude to be content under any circumstance. As we closed our prayer time, Russ began singing, "We Exalt Thee." We all joined in unity, worshipping our heavenly Father, whom we cry out to as "Abba Father" (Galations 4:6-7, which just so happens to be my Awana verse for tomorrow!).

I visited Grandma and Papa and saw the new floor on the addition. It is starting to look like something now! I also helped Dad take the gutter and fascia down from the front of the house.

Nick and I enjoyed some Arby's shakes after school!

3/9/17

Philippians 2:5-7 "Let this mind be in you which was also in Christ Jesus, who, being in the form of God, did not consider it robbery to be equal with God, but made Himself of no reputation, taking the form of a bondservant, and coming in the likeness of men."

The first part of this Awana verse jumped out at me. What was Jesus thinking when He became a man? What were His thoughts as He walked this earth? Clearly, the Bible answers these questions and more. How wonderful it is to know His mind, His Word, to have His Spirit in us!

Philippians 2:2 "Fulfill my joy by being likeminded, having the same love, being of one accord, of one mind."

Matthew 11:29 "Take My yoke upon you and learn from Me, for I am gentle and lowly in heart, and you will find rest for your souls."

John 13:12-17: Jesus our Example
"So when He had washed their feet, taken His garments, and sat down again, He said to them, 'Do you know what I have done for you? You call Me Teacher and Lord, and you say well, for so I am. If I then, your Lord and Teacher, have washed your feet, you also ought to wash one another's feet. For I have given you an example, that you should do as I have done to you. Most assuredly, I say to you, a servant is not greater than his master; nor is he who is sent greater than he who sent him. If you know these things, blessed are you if you do them.'"

Prayer: Lord, let this mind be in me, which was also in Christ Jesus! Amen.

Today I delivered mail to Daniela. Her husband, Peter, passed away around 7/16. I used to pray for them as I delivered their mail, for many months. Daniela asked me, "Jon, how are you doing?" I said, "I'm hanging in there," and handed her the mail. I delivered the neighbor's mail and Daniela approached me. "Jon, is there something I can pray for you?" I told her about Camille's situation (cancer). Daniela asked if she could put her hand on me and pray, so she prayed for me right there, and for Camille too. She asked God to fill us both with His peace and for us to have a great vacation! This is the third time a customer has asked to pray for me! What a privilege it is to be lifted up by our brothers and sisters in the Lord.

1 Corinthians 1:26-27
"For you see your calling, brethren, that not many wise according to the flesh, not many mighty, not many noble, are called. But God has chosen the foolish things of the world to put to shame the wise, and God has chosen the weak things of the world to put to shame the things which are mighty;"

2 Corinthians 12:9   God told Paul this!
"And He said to me, 'My grace is sufficient for you, for My strength is made perfect in weakness.' Therefore most gladly I will rather boast in my infirmities, that the power of Christ may rest upon me."

Colossians 1:11
"Strengthened with all might, according to His glorious power, for all patience and longsuffering with joy;"

Ephesians 3:16
"That He would grant you, according to the riches of His glory, to be strengthened with might through His Spirit in the inner man,"

Wait on the Lord in quietness.

Isaiah 30:7, 15
"...Rahab-Hem-Shebeth" (Their strength is to sit still.)
"For thus says the Lord God, the Holy One of Israel: 'In returning and rest you shall be saved; in quietness and confidence shall be your strength.'"

Psalm 84:5
"Blessed is the man whose strength is in You, whose heart is set on pilgrimage."

JEFF'S CABIN
7/4/15 - 7/9/15

I'm leaving on a jet plane to Colorado on July 4th with Brandon and Nick (my sons) and Peter and Andrew Johnson. We will meet up with Jeff, Jennifer, Nathan, and Hannah at the Denver airport and travel to Jeff's cabin in Fort Garland!

7/4
It was raining hard as we got to the cabin. Jeff and Jennifer had all the tents set up for us! They had to buy a new tent because a rat had chewed through the storage locker and eaten the tent. The rat was nursing three babies. Jeff shot her.

7/5
Breakfast: 36 eggs, 2 bell peppers, 1 onion, 1 avocado, salsa, cheese, 20 tortillas, muffins, juice, and oranges! Yummy!

I have nicknamed the outhouse that Jeff built "The Visitor Center." I think the name is sticking. We enjoy putting graffiti on the walls as we "do our business," such as "Mr. Hyatt was here" or "bombs away!"

Jeff and Jennifer sleep on a Murphy bed that Jeff built in the cabin. Andrew, Hannah, and Nathan sleep in the loft. Nick and Peter sleep in one tent, and Brandon and I sleep in another.

Psalm 119 has 22 eight-verse stanzas and 176 verses of prayers. Meditation is mentioned eight times!

Vs. 78: "Oh how I love thy law! It is my meditation all the day."

Vs.148: "Mine eyes anticipate the night watches, that I might meditate in thy word."

Counterfeit meditation, transcendentalism, mysticism: The world clearing one's mind of all subjects and allowing the mind to wander.

True meditation involves pondering, with awe, God's truth and all His ways and works, with thanksgiving and prayer!

We visited Gator Farms and got to feed alligators and even hold a two-year-old alligator.

We went to the Great Sand Dunes National Park and scaled many dunes!! We got caught in a thundershower as we entered the park, so we ended up eating our lunches in the lobby, by the bathrooms. We took turns sledding down the dunes! It was quite the workout. The wind was fierce, and I felt like I was a stucco house getting sand blasted!!

Our campfire only lasted an hour before the rains came in, but we still got to enjoy some barbeque chicken. (I had helped Jeff assemble his new barbeque the day before.)

7/6

Brandon worked hard installing steps for the cabin, with truckloads of rock and five-gallon buckets full of gravel. It looks really nice! As Brandon says, "It really adds to the value of your property, Jeff. How much do you think it would have cost to have this professionally done?" Jeff says, "Ah, around $120 since I have the supplies and I just need the labor."

I helped some with the steps and did some tree trimming. It is so fun cutting branches down and not having to pick them up! I even pushed a dead 30-foot tree down!

7/7

I cooked breakfast: two boxes of pancakes, 18 eggs, and four boxes of bacon! I had to put chocolate chips in the pancakes for Jeff and his family.

It rained most of the day, so we visited the Fort Garland Museum. Kit Carson was the General Commandant there from 1867-1868. This is a very cool place with a lot of Ute Indian, Spanish, Buffalo Soldiers, Settlers, and Civil War history. I want to bring Papa (my Dad) up here!

Psalm 119:30
"The entrance of Thy words giveth light."

Genesis 1:3
"Let there be light." God's first spoken words.

Jesus Christ is spiritually the Light of the world.

John 8:12
"Then Jesus spoke to them again, saying, 'I am the light of the world. He who follows Me shall not walk in darkness, but have the light of life.'"

7/8

We visited Pikes Peak, 14,410-feet elevation! It was beautiful!! It took us over an hour to drive to the top of the summit. There is an old cog train up top which used to haul stuff up and down the mountain. We enjoyed the views and hung out in the gift shop/restaurant when we got too cold. Outside, near the edge of the outlook, is a memorial inscribed with the words for, "Oh beautiful for spacious skies..." The writer was inspired to write this anthem after visiting Pikes Peak.

MEN'S RETREAT
10/18/19 – 10/20/19

Gentlemen,

Camille asked me, "Jon, how was retreat?" If I could sum up retreat in one word, it would be *exhilarating*. I literally was made cheerful and joyous: cheerful to be in the company of great men of God, and joyous to be joined with these men of God, in one accord, glorifying our Lord. Friday night, I had some great conversations with Pete and many of these men. Yes, we often joked and prodded each other in love, but, more often than not, we just made ourselves available to each other. I realized early on that these were divine appointments. Most of us men did not have an agenda other than just being there. I enjoyed our little group of men having the run of the camp, like Randy, Don, Carl, and I squaring off against each other at ping-pong, billiards, air hockey, and foosball in the game room Friday night. Early Saturday morning, coffee breaks amongst friends were most welcomed. As always, we also had great food and fellowship.

Our meetings were typically one hour, in the mornings and evenings. We worshipped. We also were filled up spiritually. The meetings themselves were not overbearing, but they did give us much needed food for thought from the Word of God. We studied Philemon and learned how to better pray for one another.

An impromptu meeting with Carl and Pastor Bob after lunch was a pleasant surprise. We would spend much of our "free time" sharing and praying together over our loved ones. What a beautiful time together!

Of course, there still was plenty of time left to play. Russ had brought up his bocce ball assortment to camp. He organized a game for the men. Paul, Bob, Ragan, Aaron, Carl, Russ and I played until the dinner bell sounded.

Saturday evening, after the meeting, several men huddled around Don's iPad to watch the Houston Astros battle the NY Yankees for the rights to the American League Championship. Like little boys, we watched each pitch with anticipation. I departed before the conclusion, but the game did not disappoint the men. It ended in grand fashion, with a walk-off homerun victory for the Astros over the Yankees.

I spent the late hours with Jeff, Bruce, Justin and his son, Jeff, at a bonfire. We relaxed and shared some stories. I left early and got lost - and on the wrong side of the fence! I followed the light from the pool and made my way back to camp. I would sleep much better this night. The previous night, I was so excited to be at retreat, I awoke at 5 AM!

Sunday morning, we worshipped and had communion together. Pete shared on John 17, along with other passages. What should our proper response be to God? When we partake of the Lord's Supper, are we sorrowful or joyful? We learned that it is both. Sorrow over our sins which our Savior suffered for on our behalf, yet joyful over our position in Christ. The Father sent his Son to prepare and to fit us for himself. We have been chosen by the Father, who has given us to the Son. He has done the work the Father has required. The Holy Spirit continues our preparations for the Father, while Jesus prepares a place for us! How amazing it is, the grace of God!

I am so thankful for the opportunity to spend this weekend with my friends and brothers in Christ. This was like a little vacation for me, and I feel pumped up! Many times at retreat, I was reminded of our dear old friend and brother, Jeremiah. Had he been there, he would have been proclaiming, "Glory!" One day soon, we will join him, and our retreat will last forever!

Jon

12

CANCER

IN SICKNESS AND IN HEALTH
5/10/18

"You need to drop everything and focus on getting better," my doctor said to me. "As long as you have food and water in the house, everything else can wait."

This past month I have witnessed my wife battling several bugs. She undoubtedly contracted these from working with sick kids at a daycare center. We guys do alright for a few days with a sick wife in the house, but after a while we simply long for her healthy return. We try in our own feeble ways to pick up the slack around the house, but life is just not the same. We long for her smile to return, and we long to even hear her voice without the cracks and coughs.

Today, as I recover from my own bug, I saw my wife smile again, and it brought so much joy to my heart. I heard her voice suddenly return, and it soothed my aches and pains. Restless nights past, back and forth, sleeping on the couch, waking up without her by my side, I found myself searching for her as I wandered about the night. Honey, your presence alone gives me comfort. I guess that is why God said, "It is not good for man to be alone." Baby, you are my Helpmate! Thank you, God, for fashioning one of Adam's bones! Yes, Lord, I love my woman; help me to always cherish our healthy days. And when sickness comes and it knocks us down, remind me to cleave to my beautiful wife. Remind me to love and to cherish her, in sickness and in health.

Looking back, I ponder: "Could this sickness have been some of the first warnings of the cancer diagnosis?" Either way, undoubtedly, God was preparing both of us for the future battle of our lifetimes.

Psalm 4:4, 8 "In your anger do not sin; when you are on your beds, search your hearts and be silent." " I will lie down and sleep in peace, for you alone, Lord, make me dwell in safety."

Dear God,
May I go to bed with a clean conscience and a pure heart and sleep in silence. I will lie down in peace and stay asleep, because you have saved me, and you alone are my protector.

1 Peter 5:6-7 "Humble yourselves, therefore, under God's mighty hand, that He may lift you up in due time. Cast all your anxiety on Him, because He cares for you."

11:30 P.M. EMERGENCY ROOM DIAGNOSIS
8/7/18

Metastatic Cancer of the Peritoneum

"God has a little trial for us," Camille says. Shock fills my heart as I ponder how our lives are changing in an instant. We somberly make our way home around 1:30 AM.

James 1:2-4 "My brethren, count it all joy when you fall into various trials, knowing that the testing of your faith produces patience. But let patience have its perfect work, that you may be perfect and complete, lacking nothing."

Two weeks of the great unknown follow, with several doctors' appointments and ER visits, with agony and anguish in my soul. I often find myself weeping in the middle of the night, crying out to God.

Gloria steps in immediately as Camille's caretaker. I return to work after one week of pure hell. My wife is in turmoil and pain, but through it all her spirit is resolved.

We end each night with devotions and hymns along with prayer. Our unity with the Spirit of God tightens, and we draw strength from His word.

FAMILY PRAYER MEETING
Recorded by my mother, Charlene

Robin organized a family prayer meeting at her house on August 10, 2018. It was awesome.

Those who attended: Dan, Charlene, Danny, Victoria, Emily, James, Nick, Tim, Mary, Robin, Uncle Bruce and Aunt Debbie.

We began by sharing thoughts on the new situation affecting Jon and Camille.

Then we sang two songs Jon requested: "I Cast All My Cares Upon You" and "For Those Tears I Died."

Robin then read the specific requests for prayer from Jon. Uncle Bruce and Aunt Debbie shared their requests for Becky and Caleb.

Most everyone prayed. It was especially special hearing Emily, James, and Nick pray.

Instead of praying, Mary asked if she could perform a dance, one she has done a few times. The dance was set to a Michael W. Smith song, "Healing Rain."

Uncle Bruce shared about his miraculous healing from stage 4 cancer. Most of us didn't know it was stage 4.

The meeting began with a sense of sadness, but ended joyful. Someone said: "Let's eat." We enjoyed some refreshments Robin provided. Then each went their separate ways.

What a blessing to have a family that loves and cares for each other and is willing to gather for prayer on a Friday night!

Love, Mom

This was the first of three prayer meetings my sister Robin hosted. Camille was too ill to attend this prayer meeting, so we both stayed home. Robin called during the prayer meeting. She put us on speakerphone, and we enjoyed five minutes rejoicing with our family and thanking them for bringing our battle before the Lord.

Slowly, our attitudes begin to change. What is God trying to teach us through this trial? We both begin to draw even closer to our Lord and Savior, Jesus Christ. More people begin to pray for us. It seems as if an army of angels are at work in our lives! We find great encouragement from our families and our church family. It often seems as if God has sent a specific person, at a specific time, to fill a specific need for us. I begin "Our Cancer Journal." In it, I have logged entries for every day someone brought us a meal, flowers, sent a card, visited, or reached out and served us in some way. Writing my thoughts, prayers, and praises down really helps me to focus on what God is teaching us and be thankful for each and every day.

Ovarian cancer is confirmed as the original diagnosis. Camille's next stop is three rounds of chemo, then debulking surgery, followed by three more rounds of chemo. We both feel like we have a fighting chance.

On 8/25/18, I attended a wedding for a young couple from our church. Camille was too ill to attend but wanted me to go for us. Camille's mother stayed home with her while I attended the wedding. I can remember feeling heartbroken inside yet resolved in trusting the Lord. During the reception, I randomly sat at one of 30 or so tables for around 300 people. There was a God-ordained moment as I struck up a conversation with a gentleman at my table. It just so happens that this man, Jim, was a chaplain for Kaiser Hospital in Clairemont, San Diego. Jim really encouraged me. He knew Camille's oncologist and said that he was Kaiser's best oncologist. He told me that it was good news that Kaiser was talking about surgery as a part of Camille's treatment. Lastly, Jim prayed for our situation. What a blessing!

On 9/5/18, Camille begins chemotherapy. Will this work? What if it doesn't work? Camille and I had received some solicited advice and some unsolicited advice in regards to her treatment. A dear friend had warned us this could happen. However, we decide that God's plan will not be thwarted by our decision regarding treatment. We make our decisions in spite of several well-intentioned people offering their opinions.

We start reading *Don't Waste Your Cancer*, by John Piper, and *The God You May Not Know*, by Dr. Jeremiah, along with the word of God. Church becomes an even greater encouragement to us! How wonderful it is to worship God with our brothers and sisters in Christ. It seems like almost every message or song is directed towards us and our situation. Looking back, I realize everything was pointing us towards Christ and His glory! God is truly in control, and we must take things day by day. Our worries and fears are fading away!

On 9/23/18, Camille is baptized! There are 155 folks from our church that celebrate with us. We all cram into the back yard of a family from our church. I can remember helping Camille into the pool while holding her arm up. She had a PIC line which could not get wet. Her arm was wrapped in plastic. I slipped, and almost went under, before catching myself. Fortunately, everything went smoothly, and Camille was baptized, minus her left arm! I jokingly asked the pastor if we should sprinkle Camille's left arm.

One of the many blessings received were three prayer quilts from three different churches! Also, the women of our church blessed Camille's socks off! Two women delivered a giant basket full of birthday gifts for Camille from various women in the church! Camille opens one gift per day. It takes her over a month to open each gift! Another dear friend spearheads Caring Bridge, a website used to coordinate meals for our family, give updates on Camille's condition, and provide a place for folks to leave encouraging messages for us.

Galations 6:9-10: "And let us not grow weary while doing good, for in due season we shall reap if we do not lose heart. Therefore, as we have opportunity, let us do good to all, especially to those who are of the household of faith."

10/4/18: Surgery is scheduled for 11/12/18! The doctors are pleased with Camille's progress. Praise God!

Romans 15:13: "Now may the God of hope fill you with all joy and peace in believing, that you may abound in hope by the power of the Holy Spirit."

Philippians 1:21: "For to me, to live is Christ, and to die is gain."

Philippians 3:7-11: "But what things were gain to me, these I have counted loss for Christ...that I may gain Christ. That I may know Him and the power of His Resurrection, and the fellowship of His sufferings, being conformed to His death, if by any means, I may attain to the resurrection from the dead."

Bottom line: Cancer loses! Cancer does not win! A believer does not lose their battle with cancer. They live Christ; they die and gain Christ!

CANCER HAS LOST ITS BATTLE WITH ME
10/18/18

Cancer lost its battle with me. Some people lose their battle with cancer because they never knew Christ. Other people, like me, have already won their battle with cancer. The explanation for this is simple: it's because we know Christ! As Christians, every day we live is Christ, meaning our whole life is devoted to knowing Him more and bringing Him glory. Christ has already fought the battle against sin and death. He has been victorious! Before Jesus died on the cross, He said, "It is finished!" (John 19:30). Notice the explanation mark. He did not say, "It is finished," with a period at the end, like, gee, I'm glad this is over. He said, "It is finished!" From that point on, even before He arose from the grave, Jesus had won! The battle was over!

The Bible is full of stories of God's power, but the resurrection of Christ Jesus tops them all. We believe this truth, yet as Christians we want to know Him even more - even if it means going through sufferings, even if it means getting cancer, even if it means to die. Christ's death on the cross has atoned for our sins, and His resurrection is our guaranteed resurrection! In this life, we live Christ, but when we die, we will gain!

Phil. 3:14, 21: "I press toward the goal for the prize of the upward call of God in Christ Jesus . . . who will transform our lowly body that it may be conformed to His glorious body, according to the working by which He is able even to subdue all things to Himself."

Glory!

John 16:33: "These things I have spoken unto you, that in Me you may have peace. In the world you will have tribulation, but be of good cheer, I have overcome the world."

10/30/18: Camille reminds me to "be of good cheer." I am amazed by her peace that passes all understanding. My wife's faith, in the midst of suffering, is a wonderful testimony to me!

THE BALD AND THE BEAUTIFUL
11/5/18

Tonight, I had the privilege of shaving my wife's head. Before I began, we joined hands and prayed: "Thank you, God, for all the great hair days you have given us. Thank you for the hair we are about to remove, and thank you, Lord, for all the hair that will grow back in the future." I slowly started clipping the scissors, gaining confidence with each pass. I used several guards on the clipper set, working my way down to the shortest level until only tiny stubble was left. The job ended with a kiss and my wife rushing to the bathroom, with me left wondering if she would laugh or if she would cry. I smiled as I heard her laughter echoing out the window to our patio hair salon. My wife is now bald, and, yes, she is still very, very beautiful! What an honor it is to be called her husband, and to love, to honor, and to cherish her, in sickness and in health.

Matthew 10:29-31: "Are not two sparrows sold for a copper coin? And not one of them falls to the ground apart from your Father's will. But the very hairs of your head are all numbered. Do not fear therefore; you are of more value than many sparrows."

James 5:7-8: "Be patient, then, brothers, until the Lord's coming. See how the farmer waits for the land to yield its valuable crop and how patient he is for the autumn and spring rains. You too, be patient and stand firm, because the Lord's coming is near."

Proverbs 4:23, 25-27: "Above all else guard your heart, for it is the wellspring of life. Let your eyes look straight ahead, fix your gaze directly before you. Make level paths for your feet, and take only ways that are firm. Do not swerve to the right or the left; keep your foot from evil."

Isaiah 30:21: "Your ears shall hear a word behind you, saying, 'This is the way, walk in it,' whenever you turn to the right hand or whenever you turn to the left."

11/10/18: Prayer meeting #2 is at my sister Robin's house. Brandon and I attend with the family.

11/12/18: Camille's surgery is a success! She spends the next three nights recovering from an eight-inch incision on her abdomen. One of Camille's dear friends spends the first night with her at the hospital. Our hospital chaplain pays us a visit, and two of our church pastors visit. I spend the next two nights by Camille's side.

12/9/18: Camille's first time at church post-surgery, after four weeks. We are so blessed by the outpouring of love from the body of Christ!

12/27/18: Chemo resumes.

2/7/19: Six months to the day of Camille's cancer diagnosis, she receives her last chemo treatment! I accompany her for this special occasion. Camille rings the chemo bell after finishing her treatment. It is finished! We both arrive to our home, finding a congratulations balloon and big heart balloon tied to our porch with a special gift from my mom and dad!

God has reminded me again and again of the prayers of His people, and not just for Camille and me, but for the whole world! Perhaps when we stand before God and the books are all open, we will behold the prayers we have all prayed over our lifetime. One day soon, we will rejoice in the Author and Finisher of our faith.

Hebrews 12:1-2: "Therefore we also, since we are surrounded by so great a cloud of witnesses, let us lay aside every weight, and the sin which so easily ensnares us, and let us run with endurance the race that is set before us, looking unto Jesus, the author and finisher of our faith, who for the joy that was set before Him endured the cross, despising the shame, and has sat down at the right hand of the throne of God."

2 Corinthians 5:9-10: "Therefore we make it our aim, whether present or absent, to be well pleasing to him. For we must all appear before the judgment seat of Christ, that each one may receive the things done in the body, according to what he has done, whether good or bad."

2/18/19: Camille gets her new dog, also named Camille! We change our dog's name to Ruby.

3/21/19: Camille's praise!!! "What a week it has been! I had follow-up appointments with both of my oncologists this week. Everything looks good! One doctor told me I'm a 'survivor' now, and the other doctor said I'm 'disease free.' I literally jumped for joy."

It is so amazing to see all that God has done in our lives these last seven months or so. Even if the diagnosis hadn't turned out the way we hoped, there would still be so many blessings in the midst of it all.

From the beginning of this trial in our lives with cancer, I have gone to battle for my wife. My weapons are God's word and prayer. His word comforts me and gives me strength for today and bright hope for tomorrow ("Great is Thy Faithfulness"). Prayer has sustained us. I personally made it my mission to tell as many people as I could about our situation. There are literally hundreds of people praying for us. Over 50 of them live on my postal route. I average 3-5 people/day asking for updates on Camille and reminding me of their prayers for us both. Even some who do not live on my route, but are friends or family of my customers, remind me of their prayers. Several prisoners are praying for us! Strangers in grocery stores have even come up to Camille and offered their prayers! Over three churches are praying. Neighbors are praying. Even nonbelievers offer their prayers to us and "good vibes." I figure that if God can open up the mouth of a donkey to speak, to accomplish His purpose, he can hear these prayers too! The Bible is full of stories of God using nonbelievers to complete His will. Pharaoh, King of Egypt, comes to mind.

7/7/19: Camille's cancer is back. We are reminded of one of Elisabeth Elliot's quotes: "Trust God and do the next thing."

Lamentations 3:22-32: "Through the Lord's mercies we are not consumed, because His compassions fail not. They are new every morning; great is Your faithfulness. The Lord is my portion, says my soul, therefore I hope in Him! The Lord is good to those who wait for Him, to the soul who seeks Him. It is good that one should wait and hope quietly for the salvation of the Lord. It is good for a man to bear the yoke in his youth. Let him sit alone and keep silent, because God has laid it on him; let him put his mouth in the dust - there may yet be hope. Let him give his cheek to the one who strikes him, and be full of reproach. For the Lord will not cast off forever. Though he causes grief, yet He will show compassion according to the multitude of His mercies."

7/26/19: Prayer meeting #3 is at my sister Robin's house. Nick, Camille, and I attend with the family.

CHEMO LAMENT
1/10/20

Why do I weep when I know what lies in store?

Why do I lose sleep when I've been done this road before?

I know Your promises and I know Your word.

I know that You love me, my prayers You have heard.

Suffering is never easy, even my Lord, Jesus wept.

He knew what must be done, His Father's will He kept.

"Having loved His own who were in the world, He loved them to the end."

(John 13:1b)

Washing the disciples feet, before dying for their sin.

He has given us an example, to do as he has done.

Bright hope for a new day tomorrow,

Risen now, God's only begotten Son!

DON'T WORRY ABOUT ME TODAY

8/7/19

Dedicated to Pastor Mike and his wife, Cuca, Foursquare Church

This morning, as I kissed my lovely bride goodbye,

She said, "Don't worry about me today."

Was it my teardrop she detected or my troubled heart she dissected?

Saying, "Don't worry about me today."

While I headed to work, the "what ifs" all seemed to lurk;

My wife is feeling weak, and our future seems bleak.

Cancer has taken its toll, and I've lost all control.

Am I her knight in shining armor, riding on my white horse?

Can I save the day, or can I change the course?

As I choked back the tears thinking about the next year,

Her voice echoed deep inside, saying, "Don't worry about me today."

The job was getting done, but, let me tell you, it was no fun.

My next stop was the church, and Pastor Mike knew I was hurt.

His hand was on my shoulder as he started to pray,

And as he finished, I found strength for the day.

Instead of worrying, I must wait.

It's not up to fate. It's up to me to wait.

Wait for who - wait for you? No. Wait for Him who carried the cross.

Wait for Jesus, and count all else loss.

Rest in the One who holds tomorrow;

Sing unto the Man of Sorrow and just wait.

When you're lying in your bed and thoughts start swirling in your head, just wait.

As you drift off to sleep, even if you must weep, just wait.

Please say a little prayer, and then give Him all your cares, and just wait.

Morning comes; remember His promises; remember His words.

Trust in the One who is waiting for His message to be heard.

Look unto Jesus and open your eyes; wait for His return and look to the skies!

Mr. Postman's Progress

Dedicated to Pete and Julie

3/3/20

You say that you count all things as loss, (Phil. 3:8)

For the all surpassing knowledge of knowing Me.

Yet you continue to carry your dross, (1 Cor. 3:11-15)

Wallowing in your pain and suffering.

Suffer now in grace, My child, sufficient for even you, (2 Cor. 2:9)

Cling to My holy promises, remember My word is truth. (Jn. 17:17)

That Day My fire shall consume all your dross, (Mal. 3:3-4)

Refining your heart pure as gold.

But until that Day, cling unto My Son's cross,

And keep on reading The Greatest Story Ever Told.

Be Still My Soul, be silent, now listen to His voice,

Joy Unspeakable awaits you, if in His word you rejoice! (1 Pet. 1:8)

With body, soul, and spirit, with all my heart, soul, mind, and strength,

Sing unto the Triune God, the Father, Son, and Spirit, you His saints.

'Here in the power of Christ I stand,' How Firm a Foundation.

Yet there at His feet I shall fall, with every tongue, tribe, and nation.

"Lord, remember me when you come into your kingdom," I hope to see you soon.

(Luke 23:42)

Thou must tarry here a while longer, I'm still working on your room.

In the Sweet By and By, 'we shall meet on that beautiful shore.'

In the Sweet, By and By, your friend death is but a door.

Shall We Gather at the River? Or keep on looking up to the skies?

Tarry now until I return, or "Assuredly I say to you,

Today you will be with Me in paradise." (Luke 23:43)

Written by Jonathan C. Hyatt

Inspiration from: "God's Grace in your Suffering," David Powlison and

"Joy Unspeakable," Dr. Martyn Lloyd-Jones

Hymns: Be Still My Soul, In Christ Alone, How Firm a Foundation, In the Sweet By and By, and Shall We Gather at the River?

Movie: The Greatest Story Ever Told, The George Stevens Production

Emergency Room
2/20/20, 3:09 P.M.

"I had my mom take me to the ER. I'm going to be at the Kaiser where I had my surgery. After work, get a shower and something to eat and them come join me." This was the text I received from my wife, Camille, while I was out on my route. This response was typical of my wife. Instead of worrying about herself, she was more concerned with my welfare and how she should break the news to me. I later learned that she had had her mom take her to Kaiser at Zion, around noon. Kaiser did a CT scan and promptly transported Camille by ambulance to Kaiser Clairemont. She arrived there around 3:30.

After I read the text, I called my supervisor and postmaster, Chuck. Chuck knew about Camille's battle with ovarian cancer and had been very supportive to me over the last year and a half. Chuck told me to bring the mail back that I had left. I raced back to the post office and headed home. I was in a little shock, but I managed to take a shower and get a bite to eat per Camille's request. I arrived at the ER at 4:30 P.M.

I was in a hurry to get back and see my wife, but I had to get processed. Fortunately, a kind security guard helped steer me in the right direction. As I walked into Camille's room, I saw her in bed with a resigned look on her face. Her mother, Gloria, also was in the room with three doctors. As the doctors told me what surgery they were recommending, I felt as if a two-by-four were hitting me across my head! At first I was a little ticked off at the doctors and questioned their diagnosis. Could they have treated Camille sooner with something less aggressive? The doctors had had a CT scan from the previous month and knew Camille's situation. The doctors informed all of us that Camille needed to be admitted and that surgery would be done the next day, and that we had time to think about it. Gee, thanks a lot, Doc. I walked out into the hallway with a big knot in my throat and proceeded to call my good friend, Pete. As I choked up on the phone, Pete calmly listened to my fears.

Hours had passed. We were still stuck in the emergency room, waiting to be transported to a hospital room. I decided to grab a quick bite to eat before the fast food joints nearby closed. I ordered a Big Carl combo from Carl's Jr. This was some much-needed comfort food. Camille and I had changed our diets due to her cancer and had been eating healthy for over a year and a half, but I felt like I needed to blow it now! As I sat down in Carl's Jr., I realized that I was the only customer in the place. Somberly, I choked down my burger, sipped my Coke, and ate my fries. I felt like I was eating my last meal. I felt guilty leaving my wife in the emergency room. Camille had not been able to eat any food all day long, and the doctors were not giving her any water, in case they did surgery that night.

Camille and I got transported to her room around 9:00 P.M. I had already decided that I would spend the night at the hospital too. I remember being so wiped out that I sprawled out on the couch in her room around 9:30 and dozed off. I would awake every hour or two and begin to weep.

On 2/21/20, the doctors came into our room around 7:00 A.M. They were nice, but I felt like they were saying, "Good morning, Hyatts. How about having some surgery now?" I peppered them with questions. They offered another alternative, which we decided to pursue. Cancer is no fun. Whatever choice you make seems like the lesser of two evils; however, our hopes get slightly elevated when the doctors agree to run another test with a specialist. Could this be God working? Could this be the answer to my tears and my prayers? No success. The test reveals that Camille is not viable for this procedure. Surgery is set for 10:30, Sunday morning. I'm sent home to get my rest.

I am in pure anguish of my soul as I make the long trek down the hospital hallways and down the elevator to the first floor. I walk by several people, wondering why they are here in this place. I make my way to the parking garage, trying my best to process what lies ahead of us. As I get into my car, I turn on my radio. My radio just so happens to be tuned in to Family Radio. I listen to the man read from Revelation 17 or so. I am angry. So far, family and friends' godly encouragement has seemed to bounce off of me, and I want nothing of it. I'm miserable, but as I continue to listen to this godly man simply read the word of God to me, it soothes my weary soul. By the time I get home, this godly man has read up to chapter 24 or so of Revelation.

Around 3:30 A.M. I awaken and lie in my bed. Psalm 23 comes to my mind. "The Lord is my shepherd, I shall not want…" I feel compelled to cry out to my Lord in prayer for my wife. So many people have brought her to the Lord in prayer in the past. How many prayers is it going to take? Of course we have always trusted God and His plan for our lives, yet we have always had a glimmer of hope that He may indeed heal Camille. I walked to the step in our family room and sat down in the dark. I started to pray. All I felt I could pray was Psalm 23. As I began to pray, I sobbed through the entire psalm. I have been a Christian for over 40 years. Most Christians know Psalm 23 by heart, and it should be no problem to recite it. This however, was different.

Psalm 23: The Lord is my shepherd; I shall not want. He makes me to lie down in green pastures; He leads me beside the still waters. He restores my soul; He leads me in the paths of righteousness for His name's sake. Yea, though I walk through the valley of the shadow of death, I will fear no evil; for You are with me; Your rod and Your staff, they comfort me. You prepare a table before me in the presence of my enemies; You anoint my head with oil; my cup runs over. Surely goodness and mercy shall follow me all the days of my life; and I will dwell in the house of the Lord forever.

As I climbed back into bed, I felt exhausted. I felt like a wet rag being rung out. Somehow, I drifted off to sleep and managed to get a few more hours of rest. When I awoke, I vividly remembered my dream. Now, I try not to put too much stock into my dreams, but this one was special. It consisted of no words. The dream was simply my wife Camille's smiling face! God had given me a few hours of peaceful sleep and I was very grateful. I decided to get a good devotional in the morning before I headed back to the hospital.

For my devotion, I read the hymn, "How Firm a Foundation," author unknown. My friend Pete had recited the first verse or two of this great hymn of the faith to me over the phone while I was at the hospital. He had even graciously sung the tune for me, upon my request. I had had coffee with Pete three days before Camille was admitted to the hospital. Pete also encouraged me to read *The Valley of Vision - A Collection of Puritan Prayers & Devotions*. Pete said, "Jon, read *The Valley of Vision*, and Jon, camp out in The Valley, while you are in the valley." Pete's encouragement that day proved to be invaluable to me on this morning. As I read, I began to feel peace about whatever God had planned for Camille and me, and for our future.

HOW FIRM A FOUNDATION-Author unknown

How firm a foundation, you saints of the Lord,

Is laid for your faith in his excellent Word!

What more can he say than to you he has said,

To you who for refuge to Jesus have fled?

"Fear not, I am with you, O be not dismayed;

For I am your God, and will still give you aid;

I'll strengthen you, help you, and cause you to stand,

Upheld by my righteous, omnipotent hand.

"When through the deep waters I call you to go,

The rivers of sorrow shall not overflow;

For I will be with you, your troubles to bless,

And sanctify to you your deepest distress.

"When through fiery trials your pathway shall lie,

My grace, all-sufficient, shall be your supply;

The flame shall not hurt you; I only design

Your dross to consume and your gold to refine.

"E'en down to old age all my people shall prove

My sovereign, eternal, unchangeable love'

And when hoary hairs shall their temples adorn,

Like lambs they shall still in my bosom be born.

"The soul that on Jesus has leaned for repose,

I will not , I will not desert to his foes;

That soul, though all hell should endeavor to shake,

I'll never, no never, no never forsake."

The following is the piece I read from The Valley of Vision.

Father, Son, and Holy Spirit

THE VALLEY OF VISION-A Collection of Puritan Prayers & Devotions

"THE NAME OF JESUS"

All-Searching God, thou readest the heart, viewest principles and motives of actions, seest more defilement in my duties than I ever saw of my sins. The heavens are not clean in thy sight, and thou chargest the angels with folly; I am ready to flee from myself because of my abominations; Yet thou dost not abhor me but hast devised means for my return to thee, and that, by thy Son who died to give me life.

Thine honour is secured and displayed even in my escape from thy threats, and that, by means Jesus in whom mercy and truth meet together, and righteousness and peace kiss each other. In him the enslaved find redemption, the guilty pardon, the unholy renovation; In him are everlasting strength for the weak, unsearchable riches for the needy, treasures of wisdom and knowledge for the ignorant, fullness for the empty.

At thy gracious call I hear, take, come, apply, receive his grace, not only submit to his mercy but acquiesce in it, not only glory in the cross but in him crucified and slain, not only joy in forgiveness but in the one through whom atonement comes.

Thy blessings are as secure as they are glorious; Thou hast provided for my safety and my prosperity, and hast promised that I shall stand firm and grow stronger. O Lord God, without pardon of my sin I cannot rest satisfied, without the renovation of my nature by grace I can never rest easy, without the hopes of heaven I can never be at peace. All this I have in they Son Jesus; blessed be his name.

The healing had begun. The healing was in my own heart and my own thoughts. My circumstances had not changed, but my eyes turned to my only hope, Jesus Christ. When did the healing begin? Was it when Pastor Nathan prayed with me, the day before? Was it on my drive home listening to the word of God? Was it weeping Psalm 23? Was it in doing this devotional? Was it in all of these things and even more? I finished my devotional and began to pack a bag for Camille with some items from home which she had requested be brought up to the hospital.

That morning, on 2/22/20, Pastor Bob paid us a visit at the hospital. I remember before Bob left, he asked if he could pray with us. Of course I gave him the green light to pray. I was pleasantly surprised, however, when Pastor Bob got down on his knees along the side of Camille's bed and took hold of her hand. Instantly I knew that I must do the same. I went to the other side of the bed and got down on my knees while holding Camille's hand. Bob prayed. I also prayed and I wept a little, but I noticed that my tears had changed. They were no longer bitter tears. They were tears of joy!

As I ushered Bob down the long hospital halls and down the elevator to the lobby, Bob reminded me of Isaiah 41:10, the righteous right hand of God. We chatted about this and I reminded Bob that God also covers me with His hand.

Isaiah 41:10 - "Fear not, for I am with you; be not dismayed, for I am your God. I will strengthen you, yes, I will help you, I will uphold you with My righteous right hand.

Exodus 33:13 - "Now therefore, I pray, if I have found grace in Your sight, show me now Your way, that I may know You and that I may find grace in your sight. And consider that this nation is Your people."

Exodus 33:17-22 - "So the Lord said to Moses, 'I will also do this thing that you have spoken; for you have found grace in My sight, and I know you by name.' And he said, 'Please, show me Your glory.' Then He said, 'I will make all My goodness pass before you, and I will proclaim the name of the Lord before you. I will be gracious, and I will have compassion.' But He said, 'You cannot see me, and live.' And the Lord said, 'here is a place by Me, and you shall stand on the rock. So it shall be, while My glory passes by, that I will put you in the cleft of the rock, and I will cover you with My hand while I pass by. Then I will take away My hand, and you shall see My back; but My face shall not be seen."

Bob and I decided that it is a good thing to be upheld by God's righteous right hand, and yes, it also is a very good thing to be covered by the hand of God as well!

A few hours later our son Brandon paid us a visit. Brandon brought me lunch! This was so nice after having eaten hospital and fast food for meals. After our visit and a few hugs, Brandon reminded me that I was going to escort him out to his car. As we neared the parking structure, Brandon placed his hand on my shoulder and said, "Dad you need to remain strong for me and the family. Remember who the source of our strength is: the Lord God our Father! Dad, I have been thinking about mom every 5 or 10 minutes, and I weep for her at times. I have even wept with my face on my wife's chest. I know you have wept over Mom a lot too. Dad, it's okay to weep, but we shouldn't stay there. God has great things planned for you and for Mom and for all of us." What a blessing it is to see my son's faith and his love for his mother and me.

A few other family and friends would pay us a visit, but Camille was pleasantly surprised by one unexpected visitor. This visitor's name was Asher. Asher was a white poodle mix therapy dog, accompanied by his handler, Melissa. Camille was thrilled when Asher came into her room. Melissa asked if Camille would like to pet him. Camille smiled and nodded excitedly that she indeed would love to pet Asher. Melissa placed him upon the bed and he snuggled up to Camille. What a blessing! This volunteer and her therapy dog made my wife's day. I took notice of this event and began to see God work in little ways through our difficult circumstances.

SURGERY

2/23/20

It is Sunday morning. I awake at 2:30 AM, after about 5 hours of shut-eye at home. I lie in bed thinking about the events of the day. Finally, unable to sleep, I get up at 4 AM and get ready. I leave at 7 AM with my bags packed for the next few days.

Pete and I text and agree to meet up at the hospital cafeteria for coffee at 8 AM. What a rich time, one hour together in fellowship. Pete even misses church and the sermon, preached by his son, our pastor. Pete gives me a book called *God's Grace in your Suffering* by David Powlison. I notice a coffee stain on the edge of the book cover. Pete tells me that the stain is his official seal. ☺

Family members and a few church family members begin to arrive around 9:30 AM. The surgery has been scheduled for 10:30 AM. This will be Camille's second surgery. We gather in the waiting room, and Camille heads to pre-op. I join her. When I return to the waiting room, I see a few more visitors, including Sandra and her granddaughter, Juliana. Sandra has brought up Jersey Mike's, chips, salsa, and guacamole, Girl Scout cookies, Cuties, and sparkling lemonade for all! She even feeds some strangers in the waiting room!

Surgery is a success! Camille recovers over the next couple of days and we check out of the hospital and return home. A couple of days later, I return to work while Camille continues to recover with the help of her mother and a home-care nurse.

I went to work on 3/2/20 depressed, not wanting to talk to anyone about Camille's condition. While on my route, I texted Camille to have a good day and I told her I loved her. As I'm delivering the mail, I began to think of the old hymn, "Savior, Like a Shepherd Lead Us." "...Blessed Jesus, blessed Jesus, Thou has bought us, Thine we are; blessed Jesus, blessed Jesus, Thou hast bought us, Thine we are."

I saw a hawk standing in a fresh pool of rainwater and I thanked God for His creation. On the next street, I looked to the skies and delighted in seeing the parting rain clouds. A ray of sunshine peaked down on me between the clouds. In that moment, I said a prayer in my heart, "God, I believe you have already healed Camille's heart, and, Lord, I still believe You can heal her body." Job 19:25- "For I know that my Redeemer lives, and that He shall stand at last on the earth."

THE ONE LEGGED MAN
3/1/20

Sunday morning, I went to church depressed. I had attended the past several weeks of church without my lovely bride by my side. As I waited in my car at the intersection, a disabled man rode his scooter through the crosswalk. I noticed that he was missing one of his legs, from below the knee. I thought about all the other drivers around me and wondered what they were thinking about this man who was missing his leg. I looked down at my own leg pressing on the brake pedal. I looked back up towards the man riding by. I wonder what this man's story is. How did he lose his leg? Was he in the military or a diabetic? Suddenly, I realized this man has a story. This man has a name. This man has a purpose. People pass us by every day and we tend to only notice the external things about them, but God, who searches the hearts of men, knows their heart too. May we learn to look at all people through the lens of our heavenly Father. Rather than feel pity on the disabled or less fortunate, may we realize that there is a person inside that wheelchair or scooter, and if we are fortunate, we just might get to know that person and hear their story.

1 Sam. 16:7B: "... for God sees not as man sees, for man looks at the outward appearance, but the Lord looks at the heart."

13

EVERLASTING REFLECTIONS

JESUS, I JUST WANT TO THANK YOU
10/11/19

Jesus, I just want to thank You, for dying on Calvary.

Jesus, I just want to praise You, for setting my spirit free.

You left Your home and Your throne from above,

Stretched out Your arms, because for God so loved;

Loved He the world that He sent us His only begotten Son.

I will glorify You, glorify Your Son, glorify the Three in One.

Amidst the storms and trials of life, with pain and suffering,

May we look unto You, Lord Jesus; may we continue to sing.

Jesus, I just want to thank You, for dying on Calvary.

Jesus, I just want to praise You, for setting my spirit free.

You have ascended to Your home and Your throne from above.

You have sent to us the Comforter, the Holy Spirit, with Your love,

Until that day we see You, when we have finished the race,

Until we sing Amazing Grace, when we see You face to face.

MY LIFE WITH HYMNS
10/12/19

Our great hymns of the faith hold a very special place in my heart. Ever since I was a child, I have loved to sing them. I can remember singing them at our Christian Missionary and Alliance Church. Our pastor would direct us, waving his hand up and down, while the piano and organ played the tunes of these great hymns. One Christmas, as a young boy, I sang my very first solo, "O Star, O Star, O Wonderful Star." I can still remember my mother being so very proud of me!

Every Wednesday at Christ Lutheran School the students would attend chapel. We would hear the pastor give a short message and sing hymns along with the great pipe organ upstairs. Most of the kids would barely sing; however, a few of us would carry the others through the songs. I was affectionately known as "John the Baptist" at my school.

As a youth, I learned more hymns while I attended Windsor Hills Baptist Church. I enjoyed singing so very much that I joined the adult choir at 13 years of age! A few other brave young people joined as well. The choir would sing once or twice a month, and we always had a Christmas cantata. Our choir became known as "Abundant Praise." Frequently, we would sing at various locations outside of church. My tenure lasted nearly 10 years with this choir.

In high school, at Helix High, I decided to join the school choir. We did not sing hymns or worship songs, but we sang and performed popular music. We also learned choreography to go along with some of the music. Every year we would have a "Pops Concert." I am so very thankful for this choir because this choir is where I met my future wife, Camille. Our senior year, I worked up the courage to ask Camille to our senior prom. Camille said yes, and the rest is history!

After we married, I joined Camille's church, Lake Murray Evangelical Free Church. Wow, what a long name for a church! I knew a little about her church since we used to attend each other's church every other week. Upon joining Camille's church, I promptly joined the adult choir. It was here where I grew even more in love with singing. Some of the men took me under their wings, and our director started noticing my potential. Before long, I was singing many solos. The first solo I sang, I can remember my hand squeezing the microphone so tightly that my hand was turning red. My voice was also shaking a little. Fortunately, my colleagues told me to look at the top of people's heads and not into their eyes or faces. This seemed to help me focus better. Our choir stayed together for 15 years during my tenure.

Today I am choir less. However, I still enjoy singing the great hymns of the faith and uplifting choruses at church. Perhaps one day I will join a new choir - if not on this earth, then on the New Earth or in heaven. I will look forward to eternally singing with my brothers and my sisters in Christ. I will also look forward to singing with my Lord and my Savior, Jesus Christ. I can't wait to hear His Voice!!!

Zephaniah 3:17: "The Lord your God in your midst, the mighty One, will save; He will rejoice over you with gladness, He will quiet you with His love, He will rejoice over you with singing."

GREAT HYMNS OF OUR FAITH
10/12/19

Below are just a few titles, in poetic form, of our great hymns of the faith.

Faith of Our Fathers, And Can it Be?

Jesus Paid it All, More Love to Thee.

Nearer My God to Thee, Sweet By and By,

Love Lifted Me, Sound the Battle Cry.

Stand Up for Jesus, Rise Up, O Men of God,

Onward Christian Soldiers, Breathe on Me, Breath of God.

Like a River Glorious, Amazing Grace,

Shall We Gather at the River? Face to Face.

Holy, Holy, Holy, Tell Me the Old, Old Story.

My Hope is Built on Nothing Less, To God Be the Glory!

I Need Thee Every Hour, In Times Like These, Jesus Saves,

O How I Love Jesus, Love Found a Way, O Happy Day!

JESUS' PRAYER
10/12/19

Scripture: John 17:1-26

The following poem is based upon Jesus' three prayers: for Himself, for His disciples, and for all believers. Many of the words in this poem come directly from Scripture, but they are in poetic form. They are not necessarily in the order Christ prayed them.

Father, the hour has come; glorify Thy Son.
I will glorify You; let Thy will be done.
I have finished the work You have given, given Me to do,
Eternal life to as many, as many as You choose.
Before the world began, You came up with this plan.
I will glorify You; now glorify the Son of Man,
Eternal life to as many, as You have given Him.
'Father, glorify Me, together with Yourself, I take their sin.

I have manifested Your name to the men You have given Me;
They have kept Your word and received it; in Me they have believed.
I pray for those You have given Me.
No longer in this world, I will come to Thee.
Keep through Your name those You have given, given Me, Your only Son,
Make them one as We are, and keep them from the evil one.

Holy Father, sanctify them, sanctify them by Your truth,
Your holy word is truth, I sanctify Myself, this is the proof,
As You have sent Me, I will also send them.
Fulfill My joy in them; this is my prayer. Amen.
All of Mine are Yours; now I come from this world.
Thine are not of this world; to them hatred is hurled.

I do not pray for these alone, I do not pray for these alone,
But for those who will believe and fall before Your throne.
Make them one as, Father, You are in Me;
Make them one in Us, so the world might believe,
You have sent Me, You have loved Me, I in them, and You in Me,
Make them perfectly one, with My glory, for the world to see,
Glorify them as You glorify Me; O Father, now I will come to Thee.

Oh righteous Father, I declare to them My name;
It is My desire that they will never be the same.
May they behold My glory, My glory You have given Me.
That they may know You as My Father for all eternity.
I declare Your name, the love with which You loved Me;
I will declare Your name, Thy love in Me, this is My plea.
You have loved Me, before We ever made this earth.
Oh righteous Father, may Our love give to them new birth!

GETHSEMANE
10/12/19

Scripture: Luke 22:41-44, Matthew 26:36-46

This poem is based on Jesus' prayer to His Father in the Garden of Gethsemane. Three times Jesus prayed to His Father while His disciples were sleeping. Many of the words from this poem come directly from the Scriptures, but they are in poetic form. They are not necessarily in the order Christ prayed them.

Jesus knelt down while He prayed, "Father, if it be Thy will,

Take this cup, take this cup away."

Thine angel appeared to Him, sent from heaven,

To strengthen Him whom Thou wouldst slay.

So He prayed in agony, in the Garden of Gethsemane;

Yes, He prayed more earnestly, "Father, I'll go to Calvary."

Thou didst pray to Thy Father in Gethsemane,

When Thou sheddest Thy blood for me,

As You fell on Your face, while praying in that place,

"O My Father, if it's possible, let this cup, let this cup pass from Me;

Nevertheless, not as I will, but as Thou will be done,

I will drink this cup for Thee."

Great drops of blood were flowing down;

His sweat was pouring on the ground,

Before He drank this cup for me.

Salvation's perfect sacrifice, Jesus' blood will suffice,

'Tis sin's payment, 'tis Thy price.

"O Father, I drink this cup for Thee,

As Thou sendest Me to Calvary."

CONCLUSION

9/5/19

Dear God,

It has been quite a long time since I wrote to you. I still have a handful of letters I wrote to you in my teenage years. When I look back on those letters, I read about my love for you. I read about my hopes and my fears. Today, 35 years or so later, not too much has changed. I still love you with all of my heart. I still trust in You. My hopes and my fears may have changed, but You have not changed. You are still God. You are still my God! You listen to the cries of my heart. Your Holy Spirit reminds me of Your grace. Your Son, Jesus, intercedes for me. Many days You come to my mind. Your songs play over and over in my head. As I walk, You walk with me. We have traveled together, over many hills, and through a few valleys. I know that I am not alone for Your rod and Your staff they comfort me. Thy Word is a Lamp unto my feet, and a Light unto my path. Yea, though I walk through the valley of the shadow of death, I will fear no evil, for You are with me! Please remind me that my cup runneth over. You have truly blessed me abundantly! Lord, I ask You to anoint my head with Your oil. Fill me with Your living water and restore my soul. When I lie down to sleep, make me to lie down in green pastures. May my last thought be of Your grace. Please give me a glimpse of Your face. Lead me besides the still waters while I dream.

Zephaniah 3:17: "The Lord your God in your midst, The Mighty One will save; He will rejoice over you with gladness, He will quiet you with His love, He will rejoice over you with singing."

Thank You, Father, for Your goodness to me. Thank You, Jesus, for Your amazing grace. And thank You, Holy Spirit; come fill my heart and change my face.

With all of Your faith, hope, and love,

Jonathan

2 Peter 1:3: "As His divine power has given to us all things that pertain to life and godliness, through the knowledge of Him who called us by glory and virtue."

Psalm 23: "The Lord is my shepherd; I shall not want. He makes me to lie down in green pastures; He leads me besides the still waters. He restores my soul; He leads me in the path of righteousness for His name's sake. Yea, though I walk through the valley of the shadow of death, I will fear no evil; for You are with me; Your rod and Your staff, they comfort me. You prepare a table before me in the presence of my enemies; You anoint my head with oil; my cup runs over. Surely goodness and mercy shall follow me all the days of my life; and I will dwell in the house of the Lord forever."

John 21:25: "And there are also many other things that Jesus did, which if they were written one by one, I suppose that even the world itself could not contain the books that would be written." Amen.

THIS IS NOT THE END

Made in the USA
Las Vegas, NV
15 January 2021